BORDER PATROL SERIAL KILLER

Conversations with JUAN DAVID ORTIZ

Table of Contents

INTRODUCTION 1

CHAPTER 1 | WHO WAS JUAN DAVID ORTIZ? 5

CHAPTER 2 | SERIAL MURDERS 15

CHAPTER 3 | AFTERMATH 23

CHAPTER 4 | PRETRIAL NOTES 29

CHAPTER 5 | TRIAL DIARY 57

CHAPTER 6 | CONVERSATIONS WITH JUAN DAVID ORTIZ 107

CHAPTER 7 | INVISIBLE WAR SCARS 147

CHAPTER 8 | THE LAW 165

CHAPTER 9 | THE DEATH PENALTY 215

CHAPTER 10 | JUAN DAVID ORTIZ'S TRUTH 225

CONCLUSION 237

ACKNOWLEDGEMENTS 261

A NOTE ON SOURCES 263

REFERENCES 265

ABOUT THE AUTHOR 277

BORDER PATROL SERIAL KILLER

Conversations with JUAN DAVID ORTIZ

Dr. Lyzza Janette

Author's Note

Some names have been changed and details of Juan David Ortiz's family have not been included to protect their privacy. This book is an analysis and portrait of Juan David Ortiz.

For Juan David Ortiz's Kids—

Your father loves you unconditionally with all his heart; you are the loves of his life, and you mean everything to him. You are your father's world. This book is for you to know the truth about your father—who he was ... and who he really is.

DEDICATION

THIS IS FOR NANCY JANETTE SANTOS—

TODAY, I AM KEEPING MY PROMISE TO YOU. THIS BOOK IS FOR YOU.

Nancy Janette Santos. *Courtesy of the author*

INTRODUCTION

Juan David Ortiz, please be cognizant that my intent in writing this book is not to inflict any emotional distress upon you. My aim is to present the facts with both precision and respect, ensuring that the narrative remains accurate and considerate.

You think you know—but you have no idea. This is the story of Juan David Ortiz. You may have seen his name featured prominently in national media coverage, but this is the first time you will truly hear his voice. Juan David Ortiz has entrusted me to reveal his truth, granting me permission to share his story. While many have speculated about him, I am the only one who has spoken directly to Ortiz, gleaning insights from exclusive interviews.

They call him ... the *Border Patrol Serial Killer*. His name is Juan David Ortiz. Ortiz's story raises numerous questions. Who was this man? Why did he commit these heinous acts? What was he thinking?

Why are we—as a society—so obsessed with *serial killers*? Why did his story capture the national media's attention? The media is all over this man. The media frenzy surrounding Ortiz piqued my interest, particularly because he is my contemporary. The term "serial killer" often conjures images of a grotesque figure lurking in the shadows.

Ortiz, however, appeared as a—normal ... **everyday** man. He "seemed" ordinary. Like everyone else, I, too, became curious. What is his story? Where did Juan David Ortiz come from? How did he arrive at this juncture? What led him to commit these heinous acts?

Several politicians asked me, "Why did Juan David Ortiz sleep with prostitutes?" We had never seen an "echelon" do this unprecedented behavior in Laredo, Texas. His story even garnered international attention, with coverage in Chinese media.

"To my wife and kids, I love u." "Doc Ortiz checks out." "Farewell," wrote Juan David Ortiz on his Facebook profile, as he lay in the back of a truck in a parking lot in the Ava Hotel, about to be appended by law enforcement.

The news of a Border Patrol supervisor being a serial killer who murdered four prostitutes shocked us all. As I pondered, I could not help but wonder: Who is Juan David Ortiz? He held a respectable job, was tall, handsome, educated, held a master's degree, was a Border Patrol supervisor, and a married family man.

Like many others, I became deeply interested in this case. From the outset, I knew this case would become infamous. From the moment I saw the district attorney (DA) speaking at his first press conference, following the capture and arrest of Juan David Ortiz (JD), I knew it was going to be ... HUGE (in Trump's voice) ... no pun intended.

I was compelled to chronicle this case. Unlike other instances, this one captivated national media attention, largely due to Ortiz's elusive behavior and evasiveness with the press.

In 2001, Ortiz was a hometown hero, a churchgoer, patriot, veteran, family man, husband, and father. He was the quintessential all-American boy for most of his life.

What made sense to Ortiz may not make sense to us, but it made sense to him in his head. JD is currently appealing his case. He wants his truth to be told and has entrusted me with revealing his side of the story—details of his untold narrative.

I felt compelled to disseminate the veracity of this case, as misinformation has been rampant. JD, I regard you as a human being, without judgment. Perhaps this is why you chose me to convey your truth.

To protect their privacy, I have omitted specific names and locations of Ortiz's family members. They have endured enough, through no fault of their own.

My interest in undertaking this book was sparked by the classic film, *Silence of the Lambs*. I found myself resonating with Clarice Starling, albeit in a more analytical and observational role. Contrary to comparisons, Juan David is not akin to Dr. Hannibal Lecter. He vehemently rejects comparisons to Ted Bundy, emphasizing their disparate criminal profiles. "I am not a sex killer, unlike Bundy, who committed acts of rape," stated Juan David Ortiz.

Two quotes from the film are particularly memorable: "A census taker once tried to test me. I ate his liver with some fava beans and a nice chianti," uttered by Dr. Hannibal Lecter. Another famous quote is, "It rubs the lotion on its skin or else it gets the hose again," delivered by Buffalo Bill.

Choosing not to wait for a traditional publisher, I valued the freedom to express our unfiltered thoughts and maintain creative control. Juan David personally edited the initial shorter chapters, eliminating inaccuracies propagated by the media.

Initially, I adopted a pen name, but Juan David convinced me to use my author name. I hesitated because I feared potential judgment based on appearance or personal identity. Criticism of one's work often stems simply from bias against the creator. People tend to critique more than they compliment. Juan David strongly advocated for the use of my doctoral title. I resisted, wary that it might set expectations congruous to a doctoral dissertation.

The title, *Conversations with Juan David Ortiz*, emphasizes dialogue over academic formality. I aimed to avoid scrutiny of my academic credentials or personal life. Misconceptions abound; I am not burdened by student loans. My goal was to present Juan David Ortiz on a personal level, revealing his mindset through diverse questioning. In *Ted Bundy: Conversations with a Killer*, Bundy discusses his fondness for socks. The book is predominantly conversational and has been adapted into a Netflix film, despite initial negative reviews. I recount observations from court hearings and trials authentically, preserving dialogue to evoke realistic conversations for readers.

Contrary to assumptions, Juan David granted no interviews or divulged information to the media. My decision to self-publish was driven by a desire for creative autonomy. Working with Juan David allowed us to articulate our perspectives freely. He personally reviewed and edited the manuscript, correcting inaccuracies disseminated by the media. This endeavor was born of passion for storytelling, not pursuit of fame or fortune. Collaborating with Juan David was both enjoyable and exhilarating.

The book cover reflects my vision; thoughts manifest into reality. I aimed to create a work kindred to *Ted Bundy: Conversations with a Killer*, infused with my distinctive style and personality. Our collaborative process involved spirited debates over content, eventually reaching consensus. Juan David's assertiveness and meticulousness are evident; he insists on accuracy and respects his professional title.

This book caters specifically to true crime enthusiasts and those curious about Juan David Ortiz. It is crucial to note this narrative is not about me. Some readers may take issue with my mention of eye contact during trial proceedings, but it remains an authentic detail. I am dismayed that a juror fixated on this aspect rather than absorbing the book's broader themes and detailed accounts. Such concerns underscore the responsibility jurors bear in capital cases; perhaps cognitive and comprehension assessments should precede jury duty.

Negative book reviews often stem from embittered individuals; happier people typically refrain from gratuitous criticism. Fortunately, freedom of speech allows me to share my perspective, and readers are free to abstain from engaging with my work. Achieving liberation from others' opinions is the ultimate freedom.

CHAPTER 1
WHO WAS JUAN DAVID ORTIZ?

Juan David Ortiz, born on May 22, 1983, in Brownsville, Texas, was raised by his single mother with the presence of his maternal uncle. Juan David attended Gladys Porter Early College High School, where he was a competitive member of the swim team. His friends referred to him as "JD," while his family affectionately called him "David."

I recall an instance when I called him "Juan," and he promptly corrected me:

JD: "It is David ... my name is David—not Juan."

JD often spoke about his challenging upbringing:

JD: "I lived in Section 8; joining the Navy was my only way out. My mother had to enlist me in the Navy a year early—on my 17th birthday."

During an encounter with his uncle, he mentioned, "I am a therapist—Licensed Professional Counselor."

On August 2, 2003, at Brownsville Airport, Juan David Ortiz was greeted by his family and friends with a *hero's* welcome. The front page of the *Brownsville Herald* newspaper featured a photograph of Juan David embracing his grandmother, under the headline "A Hero's Welcome." Ortiz was celebrated as a hometown hero.

On August 11, 2004, Ortiz married his high school friend, Daniella, in Brownsville, Texas.

While residing in San Antonio, Ortiz enrolled at American Military University (AMU), where he earned a bachelor's degree in criminal justice. AMU is a private, for-profit online university. He also attended classes at Saint Mary's University in San Antonio and was awarded a master's degree in international relations in 2013.

JD: I would drive alone from San Antonio to Cotulla and back.

Author: Did you have a Border Patrol dog?

JD: I was not a canine handler, nor did I have a service canine. I had a pet; the dog did his job ... to be a guard dog.

Special Agent Juan Benavides, in charge of the U.S. Customs and Border Protection's Houston Office of Professional Responsibility, stated, "There was nothing in Ortiz's record to indicate he would kill four women."

FEBRUARY 9, 2024

JD: Many of the statements Jerry Solis made about me to *Texas Monthly Magazine* are completely false. Also, I was not an Intel Supervisor.

RESUME 1—Verbatim as per Juan David Ortiz

Gladys Porter High School:

Swimming, Track, Cross Country

Youth Alive Christian Club - President

Navy / 2001 - 2009 / Honorably Discharged

Rate: Hospital Corpsman

2002 - 2005

Duty Station: 1st Marine Division Detachment, Twentynine Palms, California

Unit: 3rd Battalion 11th Marines

Deployments: Operation Iraqi Freedom (OIF I), 2003

Okinawa, Japan, 2004 – concussion

w/hospitalization

Thailand, "Cobra Gold", 2004

2005 - 2009

Duty Station: Defense Medical Readiness Training Institute, Fort Sam Houston, San Antonio, Texas

Instructor: Combat Casualty Care Course / Pre-Hospital Trauma Life Support Course

United States Border Patrol / 2009 - 2018

2009 - 2015 / Border Patrol Agent

Cotulla Station

2015 - 2018 / Supervisory Border Patrol Agent

Laredo North Station

Arrest: September, 2018

RESUME 2—Verbatim as per Juan David Ortiz

United States Navy

2001 - 2009, Honorable Discharge

Rate: Hospital Corpsman

Naval Basic Training, Great Lakes, Illinois, 2001

Hospital Corps School, Great Lakes, Illinois, 2001

Field Medical Service School, Camp Del Mar, 2002

Basic Instructor Course, Lackland Air Force Base, San Antonio, Texas, 2005

Duty station: 2002 - 2005

1st Marine Division Detachment, Twentynine Palms, California

Unit: 3rd Battalion 11th Marines

Deployments: Operation Iraqi Freedom (OIF I), 2003 -

Combat Action - returned to CONUS aboard

USS Dubuque, LPD 8

Okinawa, Japan, 2004 - concussion - off duty

Thailand: Cobra Gold, 2004

Duty Station: 2005 - 2009

Rate: Instructor

Defense Medical Readiness Training Institute, Fort Sam Houston, San Antonio, Texas

Instructor: Combat Casualty Care Course, C-4 Camp Bullis

Pre-Hospital Trauma Life Support Course

United States Border Patrol

2009 - 2018

Duty station:

Cotulla Station

Border Patrol Agent, Patrol Agent

2009 - 2015

Laredo North Station

Supervisory Border Patrol Agent (SBPA)

2015 - 2018

Juan David Ortiz—A Hero's Welcome. *Courtesy of Juan David Ortiz*

Juan David Ortiz in the Navy. *Courtesy of Juan David Ortiz*

Juan David Ortiz when he worked for Border Patrol. *Courtesy of Juan David Ortiz*

CHAPTER 2
SERIAL MURDERS

Juan David Ortiz, a 35-year-old man standing approximately six feet tall and weighing around 200 pounds, possessed black hair, brown eyes, and a military-style haircut. On the evening of September 2, 2018, Ortiz picked up 29-year-old Melissa Ramirez on San Bernardo Ave, where she had worked for nearly a decade. Ramirez entered Ortiz's truck, and they drove off together.

Ortiz took Melissa to procure drugs from a stash house, where they encountered Erika Peña, another sex worker, accompanied by a different man. They also made a stop at a store to buy some Taki chips. Melissa, a mother to a seven-year-old daughter and a three-year-old son, resided with her mother and children in a green mobile home in Rio Bravo, Texas.

In his testimony, Ortiz recounted that Melissa passed out in his truck after consuming the drugs they had acquired. Unsure of what to do, Ortiz considered taking her to the hospital but feared the surveillance cameras would reveal his identity. Instead, he began driving towards a checkpoint, eventually diverting onto a remote dirt road 24 miles north of Laredo. During the journey, Melissa awoke, insulted Ortiz by calling him a "pendejo" (stupid), and requested to urinate. Melissa got down on her own from JD's truck to urinate. As she squatted, she fell back, prompting Ortiz to lose his patience. He then shot her three times in the head and once in the right wrist. At the time of her death, Melissa was wearing black shorts and a light shirt.

Following the murder, Ortiz returned home to his "lovely" wife and children, as he later confessed. The next day, a rancher discovered Melissa Ramirez's body lying face down at the same spot where Ortiz had executed her. After receiving a call from the rancher with the aforementioned, around noon, the Webb County Sheriff's Department dispatched a deputy to investigate, finding Ramirez clutching a bag of M&M's and surrounded by .40 caliber bullet casings, indicating she had been shot at point-blank range.

Ramirez's body was transported to the county morgue, where she was identified through her fingerprints. After a few days of investigation, the Texas Rangers and Webb County Sheriff's Detectives gathered the names of three men associated with Melissa. The investigators visited the South Texas Border Intelligence Center, which coordinates with local, state, and federal agencies involved in border security. They requested license plate checks on vehicles photographed in the vicinity where Melissa's body was discovered. However, no border patrol cameras were present at the crime scene.

Ortiz, one of the center's intelligence supervisors, was asked to assist with the investigation into Melissa's murder. What was Ortiz contemplating ... knowing that he was investigating the murder that he had committed himself? Was Ortiz aghast about getting caught or did he assume he could trounce the investigators?

As Ortiz and his team conducted license plate checks, they found no connections to the three suspects. They did identify a vehicle belonging to a police officer, who explained he had been viewing property in the area and was consequently cleared. Despite the ongoing investigation, no progress was made due to Ortiz's involvement in the investigation.

Ten days later, on September 12, Ortiz picked up 42-year-old Claudine Anne Luera, a mother of five, on San Bernardo Ave. Claudine requested that Ortiz take her to the location where Melissa Ramirez's body had been found. She later confronted Ortiz, accusing him of murdering Melissa Ramirez. When Claudine exited his truck, Ortiz shot her once in the head.

The following day, Claudine was discovered on a dirt road less than two miles from where Melissa's body had been found. She was dressed in a pink sweater and blue jeans, with a .40 caliber bullet casing lying nearby. Claudine was transported to the hospital, where she died after a few hours. Before passing, she attempted to speak and requested water, expressing her thirst.

Approximately 36 hours later, on the evening of September 14, 27-year-old Erika Peña was walking on San Bernardo Ave when a white Dodge Ram truck picked her up. Erika knew the driver, whom she liked and referred to as David. Ortiz drove Erika to his home, explaining that his wife and children were out of town for the weekend. Erika said the house seemed empty and sat down to use heroin at the dining room table, with Ortiz sitting beside her.

Erika asked David if he heard about what happened to Melissa, and she stated he started to act weird. She claimed she heard the voice of her deceased boyfriend urging her to leave. Feeling nauseated, Erika ran outside and vomited on the porch. Ortiz cleaned the mess with a garden hose and suggested she eat something, prompting them to return to his truck.

Ortiz stopped at a gas station to buy her food, handing her a $100 bill. Erika purchased a Gatorade, cigarettes, and a Tally beer for Ortiz. She returned to the truck, giving Ortiz his change and the beer, while keeping the Gatorade. Erika left her pink makeup bag containing heroin paraphernalia in the backseat of the truck. When she brought up Melissa Ramirez's murder again, questioning Ortiz if he was involved, he became triggered.

David pulled out a black .40 caliber semi-automatic pistol and aimed it at Erika. He grabbed Erika's shirt as she opened the passenger door. Erika managed to slip out of her shirt, leaping out of his truck shirtless and clad only in her bra.

Erika saw a DPS trooper parked at a different island pumping gas. She ran towards the trooper, exclaiming that a man was trying to kill her, her chest heaving as she breathed heavily. Erika seemed terrified at that time. The trooper placed Erika in the back of his car, reassuring her that she was safe and could be the one to crack open the case of Melissa Ramirez and Claudine Luera.

The trooper took Erika to the Webb County Sheriff's Substation, where Texas Rangers and sheriff's detectives arrived to question her. Erika recounted everything she knew and accompanied them to identify David's house, easily locating it due to the vomit stain she had left in the front parking garage. A property search revealed the house belonged to Juan David Ortiz, a Border Patrol agent.

Believing Ortiz might flee Laredo, authorities issued a BOLO—"Be on the lookout"—message for him. Ortiz had returned home to retrieve more ammunition before heading back to San Bernardo Ave, a location investigators had not anticipated.

David picked up 35-year-old Guisela Hernandez and drove her up Interstate 35 for twenty minutes before stopping at an overpass. He told her to get out of the truck. David revealed to Guisela that he was responsible for the killings and instructed her to go to San Antonio or return to Laredo. Guisela responded, "God loves you and God forgives everything." This triggered David, who shot her twice in the neck, seemingly provoked by the mention of God or her failure to follow his immediate instructions.

David then drove back to San Bernardo Ave. There, sex worker Stephany Gonzalez, who was with Janelle Ortiz, felt uneasy when Ortiz pulled up. She told him she wasn't working, but Janelle got into his truck, and that was the last time Stephany saw her alive.

David picked up Janelle Ortiz, a 28-year-old transgender woman with no relation to him, and drove her fifteen miles up the Interstate. During the drive, Janelle knowing she was going to be executed, put her hands on her face and repeatedly muttered, "No ... no ... you are him ... aren't you?" *She didn't put up a fight*. David pulled over; Janelle got out of the pickup. Ortiz instructed her to move to the side—since she was too close to his truck—and walk behind a pile of nearby gravel; David proceeded by shooting Janelle in the back of the head.

In less than two hours, Juan David Ortiz had executed two women. Undeterred, he returned to San Bernardo Ave for the fourth time that night.

David stopped at a Stripes Convenience Store to use the restroom. He left his pistol in his truck and parked in front of the dumpster, which was located to the left of the store parking lot—not in the front of the store.

Alerted by BOLO, a DPS trooper saw David's truck—and tried to stop David as he came out of the store.

The trooper yelled at Ortiz, "Turn around ... put your hands up." Coming out of the store, David said, "You are freaking me out!" Ortiz was shocked. Another officer yelled, "Stop ... is this your truck?"

"This truck is matching the murders that have been happening!" Another officer had arrived and tried to tase Juan David ... but failed. Ortiz ran to an empty—abandoned property. The abandoned property was cleared, and they moved on to the parking lot.

David dashed towards Ava Hotel, surpassing all others in his path. Hastening toward the elevator, he harbored a desperate intention to plunge four floors to his demise through the elevator shaft as soon as its doors prematurely parted. In a poignant twist of fate, David sought to take a fateful stride forward, cascading multiple stories and ultimately meeting a tragic end atop the elevator. His state of mind was profoundly suicidal during this episode.

David ultimately hid in the bed of a truck in the hotel's parking garage. There, he posted two messages on his personal Facebook page: "To my wife and kids, I love u" and "Doc Ortiz checks out. Farewell." Ortiz remained in the truck bed for nearly an hour.

A SWAT team member found David at 2:34 a.m., handcuffing him and confiscating his keys and cell phone. Ortiz was not read his Miranda rights during the arrest but cooperated by informing officers of his pistol's location in his truck. He even suggested a SWAT member, a war veteran, take his *trophy shot*. The operation apprehension took 2 to 2 1/2 hours.

The timeline of the operation was as follows:

- 12:07 a.m.: BOLO issued.

- 12:57 a.m.: His truck was spotted.

- 1:02 a.m.: Ortiz was confronted.

- 2:30 a.m.: Located truck.

- 2:48 a.m.: He arrived at the substation.

- 3:21 a.m.: Interrogation began. Juan David Ortiz refused to speak to the lead investigator. After hours of interrogation, he confessed.

- 12:00 p.m.: Interrogation ends.

Following his confession, he was given a Whataburger meal and requested a picture of his wife and children, along with a plea not to disturb his kids' rooms. Ortiz claimed **he was cleaning the streets of Laredo ... since the police were not doing their job.** Juan David Ortiz knew the first two victims personally, but he did not know the last two. He fits the profile of a "mission-driven killer," with a specific goal that night to eliminate all the prostitutes he encountered. Ortiz had no prior criminal history. The discovery of the last two bodies occurred only after he confessed to the murders.

One might wonder if Juan David Ortiz ever reflects on his actions with regret, asking himself, "What the fuck was I thinking?" Despite his heinous crimes, there remains a possibility that he retains some vestiges of his former self. Ortiz had led an exemplary life until he began a downward spiral from February 2018 to September 2018.

I wonder if Juan David Ortiz ever thinks to himself, "What the fuck did I do? What was I thinking?"

During this period, Ortiz began taking medications for PTSD and started soliciting sex workers. It raises the question of whether these behaviors are coincidental or interconnected. Did one cause the other? Between September 2 and September 15, 2018, Ortiz embarked on a killing spree, indicating a sudden and severe psychological break.

Ortiz's own statements reveal a complex narrative. He claimed, "I was not barricading myself... I had my phone in my back pocket—I was going to reach for it so you would think I was reaching for a weapon. The reason you all didn't shoot me is because you all knew I didn't have a weapon." He also mentioned his psychiatrist at the VA, Dr. Shankar, who rapidly increased his medication dosage. "Dr. Shankar kept increasing my dosage; he's a psychiatrist at the VA—here in Laredo. He just saw me... I told him I had PTSD... and he gave me the medication—like here you go, all fast. I saw Amparan—for therapy—from San Antonio online."

Ortiz had contemplated suicide, planning to shoot himself behind Walmart on San Bernardo Ave. That night, he was suicidal and had not intended to kill Guiselda Hernandez. He wanted her to send a message that he was responsible for the killings. However, he changed his mind at the last moment.

Ortiz's background is marked by tragedy. His biological father committed suicide—by shooting himself in the head with a 38 revolver— when Ortiz was in middle school, and his parents had separated shortly after his birth.

CHAPTER 3
AFTERMATH

District Attorney (DA), Isidro "Chilo" Alaniz stated on KGNS news when the 4th body was found, "This was indeed the work of a serial killer." The authorities received a tip from a male informant—stating Claudine may have known Melissa's last whereabouts. The officials put out a BOLO—that information came across Supervisor Juan David Ortiz.

On September 15, 2018, Juan David Ortiz was qualified as a "serial murderer" by Isidro Alaniz, Webb County's district attorney. In a press conference on Saturday, DA Alaniz said, "We have probable cause to believe that he is responsible for this series of murders, which I would qualify as a *serial murderer*." Alaniz officially labeled Ortiz a "serial killer."

The case of Juan David Ortiz has been compared to the narrative depicted in the film *No Man of God*, where Ted Bundy converses with FBI agent Bill Hagmaier. Bundy remarked, "This is a person—that we're looking for here, assuming that it's just one person. This is a living, breathing, viable human being who's just going about his life in a way that makes sense to him. He is not some kind of *monster*... because he wasn't at the beginning. He's sick... *demented*... sure... but when you start using jargon like that for those impassioned terms, you forget that there's a lot of him that's in you. There is nothing that this guy has thought that you haven't thought of one time or another."

"Still avoided detection ..."

"Either vulnerable victim class like prostitutes ..."

   "Going back to the same area even when all hell's breaking loose ..."

"All of the girls being fully aware of what was going on—He still managed to get back victims."

"You know they think I'm crazy ... I'm tired of people saying I'm crazy. I'm tired of psychiatrists and some of your FBI *prima-donnas* saying that you have to have some sort of complex in order to kill people. Normal people kill people."

—*Ted Bundy*

The parallels are stark: Ortiz evaded detection despite targeting vulnerable victims, repeatedly returning to the same area even amidst heightened alert. His victims were aware of the danger, yet he continued to find opportunities.

A Spanish-language article published in *El Mañana de Nuevo Laredo* stated the following:

"Revenge due to the spread of a sexually transmitted disease could have been the trigger for the anger of Juan David Ortiz, the serial killer who ended the lives of four people—whom he picked up from San Bernardo Avenue to kill with separate bullets to the head." Ezequiel Ortiz, the brother of Humberto Ortiz, a transgender individual murdered by the Border Patrol supervisor, said in an interview with a media outlet that his brother did not deserve to die in this manner. He added that the federal agent "was cleaning" San Bernardo because he was infected with a sexually transmitted disease—and therefore—was taking revenge. Although the authorities have not officially revealed the motive for the homicides, it emerged that Ortiz was infected with the HIV that causes AIDS, as he frequented San Bernardo Avenue to pay for sex.

The federal agent discovered that he was infected, and this revelation triggered his anger against the people who sell sex on San Bernardo Avenue. However, the district attorney's office indicated that these claims were merely speculative. "But Ortiz was as healthy as you or me. Condoms were found in his truck," Alaniz stated.

According to the *Texas Monthly Magazine*, Laredo criminal defense attorney Joey Tellez, who was initially appointed to represent Ortiz, said that Ortiz told him that a VA doctor had diagnosed him with PTSD in February 2018. Tellez said that Ortiz also claimed that the drugs the VA doctors prescribed him had "messed him up." Ortiz told Tellez that when he was arrested in the parking garage, he had shouted, "The VA did this to me." According to Tellez, Daniella was distraught that she had encouraged her husband to see a doctor at the VA clinic. She had come to believe that the medications he was prescribed—had caused his troubles. Joey Tellez went to the *Texas Monthly Magazine* to speak about Juan David Ortiz's case.

Marcela Rodriguez, Erika Peña's aunt, established a GoFundMe page to raise $20,000 for Peña's medical and legal expenses. The campaign successfully raised $10,202. Rodriguez issued the following letter:

"I want the community to know that she really needs the help, Rodriguez said. As you may have heard, Erika Peña, (mother of a 5-year-old daughter) was the fifth victim that was able to escape the serial killer. Unfortunately, this resulted in Erika having extreme trauma.

We are currently struggling to afford the expenses and the required resources to get the help that Erika needs for her to be able to recover from this very unfortunate and horrific event.

I, Marcela, am representing my niece and am asking for any generous donation to cover psychological/medical and lawyer expenses.

Thank you,

Marcela Rodriguez"

A Facebook post from Erika Peña read: "Pantaloncito nuevo y tacones nuevos. Lista para la calle." Translation: "New pants and new heels. Ready for the streets."

Laredo Morning Times documented Erika Peña's apprehension while under the influence of narcotics. The article raises concerns regarding the allocation of the $10,202 donated by the public. Given that this sum represents the hard-earned money of the contributors, it is imperative to investigate and understand how these funds were utilized.

According to Marcela Rodriguez, Erika agreed to accompany Ortiz to his house in Laredo, Texas, on September 14, after he offered her $500 for sex.

Author: Did you pay Erika Peña $500?

JD: No, that's not true. I never paid her $500. There are many false stories about me, and most of them are not true. Don't believe everything you hear. This is why I'm telling you my truth—so you can put it out there in your book.

Erika initially described him as "cheerful" and "talkative." Prostitutes on San Bernardo Ave are typically paid $20 to $30 for sexual acts, depending on the service.

Ortiz's Confession (Verbatim):

"Anna Gabriella Hernandez ... I only picked her up once. She asked me to buy her 'medications' in Mexico, and I told her—no. Then she told me she was going to Dallas to move her stuff. That was the last time I picked her up. She dropped her phone and called her cell—that's how she got my number. She kept texting me, so I blocked her."

MARCH 21, 2024

"JD: What Anna Gabriella (Anna Karen) said about me to the media is not true."

"The author recalls encountering an Assistant District Attorney (ADA) following Ortiz's confession but prior to initiating communication with Ortiz. For the purposes of this discussion, we will refer to this former ADA as 'John.'"

John: JD confessed and doesn't have an attorney yet. He is just there without legal representation. He will be charged soon. He wanted the "girlfriend experience." I'm being seduced by an author to reveal details. LOL.

"The author contends: JD was on suicide watch, and I kept hearing stories from friends who worked at the Webb County Jail. I requested that Father Harris visit JD to check on his well-being, as JD had no family in Laredo and was not a local resident."

Ortiz is the type who meticulously reads manuals and files grievances, resembling a mini-lawyer. He would have been considered a nerd.

Memes began circulating, especially since it was close to Halloween.

Meme Exchange:

Border Patrol Agent: Are you a U.S. citizen?

Person at the checkpoint: Are you a *serial killer*?

Another meme featured a border patrol agent wearing a Michael Myers mask.

After JD called me, I noticed a Sheriff's truck pass by my house as I was leaving. I stood there and stared at the two officers, with nothing to hide. Attempting to write a true crime book is not illegal, as far as I know.

CHAPTER 4
PRETRIAL NOTES

JANUARY 10, 2019

Juan David Ortiz appeared in the 406th District Court for his arraignment hearing, wearing a faded orange uniform. He scanned the entire room, focusing on those in the back. Ortiz pleaded "Not Guilty" to capital murder and other charges. An initial pretrial hearing was scheduled for April 25, with a second hearing set for October 3.

Joel Perez orally petitioned for Raymond E. Fuchs to join Ortiz's defense team as co-counsel. Upon exiting the courtroom, Melissa Ramirez's mother vociferously exclaimed in Spanish, "Maldito asesino!"—translated as "Damn murderer." Ortiz retorted with a sinister smirk. The courtroom, filled with a tumultuous atmosphere, fell into a stunned silence, shocked by the outburst. Ortiz turned towards the exit, momentarily pausing to incline his head in acknowledgment towards me, a gesture of salutation. Earlier, I had observed Ortiz bowing respectfully to his attorney.

A reporter seated behind me asked if I was related to Juan David, having noticed his gesture of respect towards me. I assumed he learned this in the military, where non-verbal communication is common. I had informed JD in a letter that I would be wearing pink glasses.

From the outset, I knew this story would gain significant attention. And sure enough, I was right. Everyone wanted a piece of it.

Interview Excerpt:

Author: Did you see me wearing my pink glasses?

JD: I didn't receive your letter; they never gave it to me ... until months later. I do remember your pink glasses; I thought you were cute and pretty. Your glasses did get my attention.

Author: I smiled at you, thinking you had received my letter and that's why you stopped and bowed your head at me.

I remember advising JD not to gaze at the families in that manner, but to maintain a direct focus. Upon his subsequent court appearance, he averted his eyes to the floor, intentionally avoiding the families altogether. The courtroom had transformed into a frenzied media spectacle, casting JD as its central curiosity.

APRIL 25, 2019

1:40 p.m.

Hearing #607116

Juan David Ortiz's Case

Pretrial Conference

Discovery was moving along, and a second chair was appointed. A bond reduction will be filed. Juan David didn't see me. Exiting, he looked downward, but upon entering, he maintained a straight gaze. Later, Juan David disclosed to me that he had recently dedicated his life to Jesus.

The prosecution's side was densely packed, and I aimed for a close-up view. The first row on the defense side was also reserved, with numerous media representatives, visibly from out of town, seated among them. As I entered, I observed the families conferring with the DA. Judge Hale's absence was noted. The mother of the initial victim sat calmly on the prosecution's side, noticeably composed compared to before. It was now 1:56 p.m., and my phone remained inoperable in the courtroom. More families of the victims arrived, dressed in shirts bearing the images of their lost loved ones.

A political party acquaintance of mine sat with the prosecution team. A relative of the second victim left the courtroom in tears. A bailiff remarked aloud, "Something seems amiss considering the time." The prosecution side was overwhelmingly crowded.

At 2:13 p.m., the court proceedings commenced. Juan David sported a shaved head and appeared heavier around the midsection. Juan David was unaware of my presence. Joel Perez addressed matters concerning the second chair. Perez filed a habeas corpus electronically. A bond reduction will be filed by Perez. "221 days in custody," Judge Hale declared. "Hearing for lowering the bond—Hearing on writ only," said Perez to Judge Hale.

OCTOBER 3, 2019

10:30 a.m.

Internal affairs personnel joined the prosecution side. Once again, my phone was nonfunctional. Perez conversed with Juan David's mother. I overheard a man inquire of JD's mother and uncle, seated at the rear, about a $30,000 check. The prosecution displayed a large poster of Erika Peña. During the court session, JD, now with short hair, wore an orange prison uniform.

A writ of habeas corpus and bond release were discussed. JD glanced at me, offering a smile, before surveying the room. His appearance seemed slimmer, with a darker complexion. The ADA and the victims' families occupied the prosecution's side.

JD's legal team contested the bond conditions. The State sought to deny bond, presenting two witnesses. Indicted on December 5, 2018, JD shook his head in disagreement when it was mentioned that Guiselda Hernandez had been struck and shot in the head.

"No drinks allowed in the courtroom," a court attendant reminded.

DA Alaniz stated, "JD has no employment or family ties in Laredo—I am pursuing the death penalty."

Erika Peña, accompanied by Federico Calderon, entered the courtroom. Peña, noticeably taller with a heavier build and blonde hair, wore large hoop earrings and a black sweater. Smiling proudly, she took an oath. Adorned with a silver necklace, she had undergone a noticeable grooming.

Erika Peña, aged 27, is the mother of a ten-year-old child who will celebrate a birthday on October 15. Her criminal history includes intermittent incarcerations, multiple convictions for misdemeanors, and ongoing legal cases. At present, Peña is undergoing rehabilitation, participating in inpatient treatment to facilitate her recovery. Her *drugs of choice* are heroin and crack cocaine.

During a statement, Peña mentioned that she has not been offered any plea agreements by the State of Texas. She disclosed that she occasionally uses benzodiazepines (bars) and has experimented with marijuana, though it is not her favored drug. Peña admitted to injecting heroin as her preferred method of consumption. Pointing towards Juan David Ortiz, she noted his attire in orange, referring to him familiarly as David, with whom she has been acquainted for approximately five months.

Erika smiled at Ortiz, and he reciprocated with a grin. She maintained her gaze on him, observing intently. Upon inquiry about the locations of Ortiz's tattoos, she responded, "Arms, chest," and speculated that he also had one on his leg.

ON MARCH 21, 2024:

JD clarified, "I do not have a tattoo on my leg."

CONTINUING OCTOBER 3, 2019

Erika purported that she observed David near Market Street. She recounted an interaction on San Bernardo Ave by the Evelyn Hotel, during which David extended an offer to give her a ride at approximately 11:00 p.m. on the first evening.

Initially working as an escort, she supported her drug addiction through sexual favors. Erika smiled while testifying about engaging in sexual activities with David. Their relationship evolved into a friendship. She hesitated but eventually entered his white truck.

"No objections," Perez, JD's attorney, interjected.

Ortiz picked her up in the same vehicle on at least five separate occasions. Peña possesses knowledge of David's residence. He transported her to his house on a minimum of two occasions. She was present at his residence in San Isidro on the night of the State Trooper debacle.

DA: "What sexual acts did you perform on Juan David Ortiz?"

Erika: "Lots of kissing, sex, and blow jobs in his truck..."

DA: "Where would Ortiz park the truck?"

Erika: "Once outside Walmart and Cactus Motel... David rented a room once or twice at Cactus Motel."

"Erika maintained a smile as she recounted, 'David would give me money to do things to him.' She described how he would escort her to procure drugs from crack houses, where he once descended to buy crack and heroin on her behalf. David facilitated her access to heroin and crack cocaine, and she proceeded to inject heroin in his presence while he observed. Shockingly, these drug rituals occurred at the dining table used by his family."

During her court testimony, Erika Peña recounted David's instructions to her to maintain a pleasant demeanor, emphasizing her favored status while disregarding her opinions. According to Peña, "David told me to be nice, that I was his favorite, and that he didn't care what I thought." She clarified, "I never 'worked' for him; he looked for me." Peña recalled an occasion where David appeared in uniform, albeit with his shirt inside out and wearing khaki boots. She admitted to frequently using drugs in his presence.

According to Erika, "David had a star on his shirt. He told me he was a Border Patrol. We talked about a lot of stuff, that he had problems with his wife, marriage problems. His wife was upset because she didn't like Laredo. He has two kids. He said that his wife was never there at his house."

Erika affirmed her acquaintance with Melissa, who met a tragic demise. According to Erika, both Guiselda and Melissa, who worked along San Bernardo Ave, were victims of murder. Erika further disclosed her familiarity with Claudine and Janelle, who similarly engaged in street work. Additionally, Erika Peña indicated that Melissa had been romantically involved with David.

ON MARCH 21, 2021:

Juan David Ortiz elucidated, "Erika did not know where I worked or that I worked for Border Patrol."

CONTINUING OCTOBER 3, 2019

Amidst the downpour, Erika ambulated, consuming heroin and crack. Clad in white tennis shoes, she clutched a floral makeup bag housing a pipe and syringe. Joel Perez observed the image and surrendered it to the prosecution. Peña's floral bag was discovered within David's vehicle; however, she was unable to reclaim it. Erika abstained from consuming beer.

David disbursed $100 to her for the acquisition of two beers, cigarettes, and a Gatorade.

Currently, David is actively transcribing notes within the courtroom.

In Clark, Arkansas, and on Lyon Street, Peña purchased narcotics. At 6:00 p.m., David picked her up. They procured drugs first, followed by beer. David was clad in a khaki shirt and jeans—the same attire he wore in custody. He collected her in his white Dodge. Erika queried David about Melissa and Claudine's ordeal.

Erika felt apprehensive due to her friends' murders, a topic of widespread discussion on San Bernardo Avenue. David mentioned seeing it on the news.

Both Melissa and Erika were romantically involved with David; however, Melissa's relationship did not unsettle Erika. Erika was aware that Melissa and David had dated on multiple occasions. Erika claimed that her relationship with David did not disturb Melissa.

Erika occupied the corner of the table, accompanied by David in his residence. Her unease heightened as she observed his abnormal demeanor. Despite her assurances, Erika concealed her fear, surreptitiously preparing heroin. David inquired about her injection site, causing further agitation and a visceral pang in her abdomen. Erika heard a voice in her head telling her to get out fast.

"Erika Peña would sit on his lap while smoking a cigarette. She was in the midst of injecting drugs. According to her, she knew what was going on. Erika refrained from sitting on David's lap as she had done before. She felt damp due to the rainy weather and vomited. She entered his truck at the street corner. David insisted that Erika needed nourishment and drove her to a nearby store close to his residence."

David brandished a firearm at her without uttering a word. Peña feared for her life, convinced that her end was imminent. With precision, David aimed the gun directly at Erika's chest, his vehicle idling nearby. In a desperate attempt, she attempted to sound the horn inside the truck. Meanwhile, David continued to wield the firearm, forcibly pulling at Erika's shirt. She fled in haste, clad only in a bra, jeans, and sneakers.

Peña encountered a state trooper refueling his vehicle, disclosing that an individual was aiming a firearm at her. JD endeavored to restrain her within his truck, inducing a profound fear of mortality in Peña. She described the weapon as black in hue to the trooper and conveyed her apprehension for her safety. Upon departure, Peña remained apprehensive of David. Erika harbored concerns that David might attempt to murder her should he be released on bail.

The trooper characterized Peña as "one of those women" in his telephone conversation. He escorted Peña to the police station. Peña divulged all pertinent details. David was aware of her residence—on Steward Street with her mother. According to Erika, she and David frequented the vicinity of her home. David visited her residence on multiple occasions. He discarded her mobile device. David would telephone Erika at her residence.

Erika detailed, "David got mad because I wanted to go and do me (meaning to keep doing what she was doing—prostitution and illegal drugs). He threw my phone out of his window."

Instructing him to procure a replacement phone, Erika emphasized her desire to return home, positing that his actions stemmed from a desire for increased intimacy, prompting him to discard her phone.

Erika: ... Like he wanted "more" and that's why he threw my phone away—

MARCH 21, 2024

David refuted allegations of pursuing a relationship beyond advising her to leave her profession for her well-being.

JD: I did tell Erika to leave that profession for her own good, as I would tell any other person—but that didn't mean I wanted to leave my wife and kids to be with her. That's not true.

CONTINUING OCTOBER 3, 2019

Erika expressed her desire to contact her mother. During a direct examination with Joel Perez, she disclosed, "I've been in rehab for 30 days voluntarily, without experiencing any drug withdrawal symptoms." Having struggled with addiction for nine years, Erika Peña, on April 15, was deeply ensnared by crack cocaine. Her daily expenditure ranged from $200 to $300 on drugs. Beginning her journey to recovery on September 2, Peña sought rehabilitation services amidst her dependence on substances such as black tar and street crack, each costing approximately $100 per dose.

In her interactions with District Attorney Alaniz's office, Peña has engaged on four occasions, with recent sessions spanning one to two hours daily across yesterday and today. She was asked by Perez if she inquired about pending charges and whether her bail had been reduced during these discussions. Following a three-month confinement, Peña continued to consume crack in the mornings and heroin throughout the day, perpetuating her cycle of substance dependence. Peña used heroin that day. She went to David's house and did more heroin.

Erika recounted hearing a male voice with a Spanish accent instructing her to leave the house. Peña underwent methadone treatment during her rehabilitation. Her child, now ten years old, resides with a family member, though Erika did not relinquish custody. She visits her child every three months. Peña alleged that heroin's effects do not induce vomiting for her. David collected her at 6:00 p.m., and they spent time driving around and consuming beer. This outing extended for a considerable duration. Erika reported to the State Trooper at 9:00 p.m., at which point she was under the influence of narcotics.

The intensity of these inquiries is overwhelming. Peña suffers from PTSD and depression, having been diagnosed within the past 30 days. To manage her symptoms, Erika is on medication. She experiences nightmares, anxiety, and panic attacks, frequently dreaming of David as a result of his actions.

12:20 p.m.

I am seated next to Investigator Calderon outside the courtroom, awaiting the resumption of the trial. Ortiz's legal representatives were consulting with his family about the possibility of appealing JD's case and moving it to a more convenient location. Marco Gonzalez is acting as legal counsel for Erika Peña.

12:35 p.m.

Fred Calderon was taken to the District Attorney's office.

1:05 p.m.

A new witness stepped forward to provide testimony, marking the beginning of a fresh start. The Sheriff appeared, and the subsequent interview proved to be intense and gruesome. Perez engaged in conversation with JD's family members, while reporters from out of town observed the proceedings.

1:17 p.m.

JD confided in me at the court that he had not received any photographs, voicemails, or letters from me. Juan David mouthed, "No me ha caído nada," indicating that he had not received anything. JD reiterated to the Sheriff's Deputy that he had not received any correspondence, and both men turned to look at me. The deputy informed me that JD had not been sent any items.

1:30 p.m.

Captain Fred Calderon was called to testify as a prosecution witness. He has been involved in criminal investigations since 2005.

September 3, 2018

Calderon received an urgent phone call reporting a deceased individual near Camino Colombia. Ernesto E.J. Salinas, an operative with the Texas Rangers, promptly arrived at the scene and conducted a thorough photographic documentation. The victim, a female, was discovered face down, clutching a yellow bag of M&M's, with a visible head wound. Amidst the somber scene, her family mourned profoundly as photographs of Melissa Ramirez, who had suffered multiple gunshot wounds and was now deceased, were displayed in the courtroom. Three .40-caliber shell casings were located in close proximity to the body.

Further investigation revealed a disturbing pattern: four murders were linked by the same firearm, a fact confirmed through meticulous laboratory analysis. The weapon in question was traced back to Juan David Ortiz.

Dr. Stern formally identified the deceased as Melissa Ramirez, noting two to three gunshot wounds inflicted at the back of her head, indicative of an execution-style killing.

September 13

A few miles from the site of the initial homicides, authorities discovered the lifeless body of a woman, her face turned downward, bearing gunshot wounds to the head.

Claudine Luera, upon making incoherent statements, requested water and subsequently expired at Doctors Hospital of Laredo.

Juan David, who possesses four tattoos, likely acquired one on his leg during his service in the Navy. In court, I expressed my disapproval by shaking my head in negation towards Juan David.

Crime Scene 2—A Subsequent Execution

September 13

September 13 marked the occurrence of the second murder.

September 14

At a gas station on Loop 20, Erika Peña alleged that David Ortiz had killed two women and drove a large white Dodge pickup truck. She described his residence, remarking its distinctive steps and the location where she had vomited in front of his house, situated northeast. Peña subsequently guided investigators to Ortiz's residence located at 204 Burr Oak, at the intersection with Chisos Oak Drive, a location verified by the Webb County Appraisal District records. She disclosed that David Ortiz was one of her clients.

In court, Calderon identified Juan David Ortiz, who was attired in an orange jumpsuit.

Erika Peña approached a State Trooper at 9:00 p.m. Ortiz was observed near the intersection of Jefferson and San Bernardo Avenue, an area notorious for prostitution. Upon realizing the presence of law enforcement, Ortiz fled on foot.

September 14

A body was discovered off IH 35. In a coordinated effort, a Ranger managed the scene and incorporated photographic evidence into the investigation. Guiselda Hernandez's body was found not far from the other two victims.

In court, Juan David Ortiz occasionally glanced at the families of the victims. Calderon was absent during the crime scene photography. Joel Perez questioned the integrity of the photographs, asking, "What if they were altered?" Guiselda Hernandez had sustained blunt force trauma, gunshot wounds, and other injuries.

Ranger Salinas reported that Ortiz fled to the Ava Hotel and was later found in a pickup truck's bed. Law enforcement had secured the area, and a .40-caliber handgun, identified as Ortiz's border patrol-issued firearm, was retrieved from the scene. The DPS Laboratory confirmed the weapon matched the shells found at the crime scenes. Calderon was seeking Ortiz on charges of evading and resisting arrest.

Ortiz exhibited indifference and agitation, initially denying involvement before admitting to the crimes. Ranger E.J. Salinas read him his rights at the outset, and Ortiz did not request an attorney from Calderon.

2:00 a.m.

Calderon commenced an interview with Ortiz, who initially denied knowing Erika Peña but eventually admitted to brandishing a weapon at her. Ortiz confessed to four murders, detailing how he picked up Melissa, took her to buy drugs, and she subsequently passed out in his truck. Although Ortiz considered taking her to a hospital, he refrained due to the presence of cameras. Instead, he stopped on Jeffrey Road, where Melissa, agitated, exited the vehicle to urinate. Seizing the opportunity, Ortiz killed her. Claudine Luera, wanting to see where Melissa had died, was also shot by Ortiz.

According to Calderon's court testimony, Ortiz remarked that Guiselda emitted an offensive odor, necessitating the lowering of the windows. He instructed her to depart for San Antonio or return to Laredo, asserting his culpability for the homicides. However, Guiselda refused to comply, prompting David to fatally shoot her.

Ortiz directed the authorities to the location of the fourth body, stating, "You all need to check it out near the area, old checkpoint off IH 35—the fourth murder." While Calderon remained to interview Ortiz, he dispatched others to locate the remains. Janelle Ortiz, identified as the fourth victim, had a projectile recovered from her body, as did the other victims.

A joint operation with the Texas Rangers uncovered a rifle and shotgun at Ortiz's home. Ortiz believed law enforcement was closing in on him. The lethal firearms, loaded with ball ammunition, were found on the kitchen counter. Ortiz was involved in the murder of Melissa Ramirez. According to Calderon, Ortiz declared, "They were nasty, mierdas (shit), jobless, not worthy, shit—that given a chance, he would get rid of all of them."

Joel Perez, JD's attorney, recounted, "The first time you saw Juan David Ortiz, he was in the back of a truck, compliant upon removal. He cooperated throughout transport and upon arrival at the interview room. He remained restrained, displaying no signs of aggression, agitation evident hours later when left alone."

CONTINUING OCTOBER 3, 2019

3:00 p.m.

At 3:00 p.m., David's mother, uncle, and friends prepared to testify on his behalf. Reporters pursued an interview, recounting their observation of courtroom mistreatment based on JD's glance toward me. A sympathetic bailiff accepted the impropriety, advising me to proceed to Judge Hale's office for resolution. Courthouse staff acknowledged the inappropriate behavior of the bailiff and assured support, ensuring the matter was addressed without media involvement.

Reflecting on subsequent events, I regret not witnessing JD's mother's testimony, expressing sympathy for her ordeal.

OCTOBER 4, 2019

The court session was scheduled to commence at 8:30 a.m., yet by 8:32 a.m., proceedings had not begun. Wayo Ruiz, an associate of Judge Hale, approached me for a conversation. Wayo exhibited genuine kindness and respect during our interaction. Moreover, he intervened on my behalf, requesting that the bailiff refrain from any further harassment.

Wayo assured me that if I encountered any future issues, I could reach out to him for assistance. Consequently, I experienced no subsequent problems. He informed me that there would be no court session today, as all matters had been resolved the previous day, which I unfortunately missed. The bond had been denied on October 3, 2019.

10:30 a.m. - 3:30 p.m.—JD's mother provided testimony, asserting her unawareness of his interactions with prostitutes. She emphasized his upbringing in a Christian household and described him as non-violent. Additionally, she expressed her willingness to assume his care if granted custody.

OCTOBER 31, 2019

Juan David Ortiz was called a *vigilante*.

FEBRUARY 9, 2020

On February 9, 2020, I received advice from a reliable source instructing me not to respond to JD's calls. Allegedly, the sheriff intended to manipulate me into appearing in an advertisement against Ponce Trevino, a former associate now contending for sheriff against the incumbent. The sheriff planned to insinuate my endorsement of "serial killers" and Trevino, exploiting JD unknowingly in the process.

I found it peculiar that JD, who had not contacted me for some time, suddenly began calling repeatedly. Following my friend's counsel, I refrained from answering. I did, however, send JD a copy of the book *Saint Paul*. Whether he received it through Amazon remains uncertain.

FEBRUARY 26, 2020

I do not condone JD's behavior. No one emerges victorious from this situation. Every individual has suffered; each person is a casualty. The families have mourned their loved ones. JD's own family has been victimized. Moreover, JD has lost his children; they too are casualties, deprived of their father's physical presence. JD met his demise in this tragic event.

I was dissatisfied with simply labeling JD as a murderer. I am inclined to seek understanding—what drove this behavior, what was its root cause? Was it PTSD stemming from warfare experiences? It is imperative that we seek solutions to this issue. JD's case is not isolated; numerous war veterans endure similar struggles. Do we require enhanced military training, improved pharmaceutical interventions, or reduced reliance on medications from major pharmaceutical corporations?

It is appropriate to hold Big Pharma and governmental entities (including the military and the VA) accountable for the harm caused by medicating both civilians and veterans. The Laredo VA Clinic prescribed medications to Juan David Ortiz, ultimately leading to these tragic events. JD exhibited no history of violence prior to these prescriptions. It was only after commencing this medication regimen that he found himself embroiled in this crisis.

The most effective means to prompt change is by targeting their financial interests—lawsuits against the government. Our current system for treating war veterans is flawed; we must provide improved care and establish mental health facilities or state hospitals specifically tailored for veterans. Families on both sides of this issue should consider litigation against the government and Big Pharma (the top 1 percent).

JUNE 29, 2020

MONDAY

On June 29, 2020, Ortiz appeared in court wearing a white face mask, a precaution due to COVID-19. This time, he sported hair and exhibited a lighter complexion, which noticeably improved his appearance compared to when he was bald. He seemed in better health overall.

Ortiz declined to sign the waiver for his 6th Amendment rights, but Calderon indicated "refused to sign" on the paperwork. Calderon assured Ortiz of favorable treatment, including a photograph of his family, advocacy with the District Attorney, and arrangements for his pension to benefit his wife and children.

Following a ten-hour interrogation, Ortiz eventually confessed, a clear violation of his rights. The DPS trooper who apprehended Ortiz could not recall others present during the arrest, lacking a valid search warrant or probable cause beyond a coworker's text message. Throughout the court proceedings, JD displayed nervous behavior, fidgeting with his hands.

Despite Ortiz's reluctance and refusal to sign the waiver, authorities persisted in questioning him, thereby further breaching his 6th Amendment rights. Mr. Perez highlighted these issues during the court hearing.

Could JD's circumstances have been different had his father been involved in his life? Perhaps if JD had not served in the military or refrained from taking medication, the sequence of events might have unfolded differently.

It is crucial not to let emotions or a desire for retribution supersede legal principles.

JULY 14, 2020

The defendant's *Motion to Suppress* was DENIED. Judge Hale ruled that Juan David Ortiz's (JD) confession would be admissible in court as evidence for the trial.

SEPTEMBER 4, 2020

District Attorney Alaniz announced his intent to seek the death penalty for Juan David Ortiz. The confession was admitted as evidence.

JANUARY 7, 2021, 3:00 p.m. - Hearing (Online)

The State asserted that Ortiz's confession is fragmented and cannot be seamlessly compiled. The defense requested access to the full confession but has been unable to obtain it. A hearing is scheduled for mid-May.

MAY 20, 2021, 9:30 a.m. - Status Hearing

Juan David Ortiz appeared immobile, seemingly heavily medicated or lethargic, not even blinking. His trial is scheduled for March 2022. The prosecution is unable to provide the defense with a complete version of the confession, only fragmented portions.

AUGUST 17, 2022

9:45 a.m.

Final Pretrial Hearing for Juan David Ortiz

The prosecution team, consisting of seven members, faced off against Ortiz's defense, represented by two attorneys.

9:54 a.m.

Judge Hale, accompanied by Wayo Ruiz, entered the courtroom. The primary focus of the hearing was the *Change of Venue* request, which Judge Hale approved, relocating the trial to Bexar County. Additionally, the *Motion to Suppress* evidence was revisited due to Deputy Calderon's involvement.

Defense attorney Perez argued that Ortiz had been coerced into confessing by Calderon and Ranger Salinas. Despite Ortiz's explicit refusal to sign any documents and his clear statement that he did not wish to speak, the officers continued to apply pressure. Perez emphasized Ortiz's invocation of his right to remain silent and his request for legal counsel, which were disregarded by Calderon and Salinas. District Attorney Alaniz countered, asserting that Ortiz never requested an attorney and would commit perjury if he testified to the contrary.

Perez interrogated Calderon regarding the execution of the vehicle inventory search. Calderon appeared visibly stunned. The defense underscored the lack of a proper inventory or vehicle search. Perez also questioned whether Ortiz had invoked his right to counsel, while DA Alaniz referenced phone calls in which Ortiz confessed to his wife.

DA Alaniz stated, "They have three videos of Ortiz entering his vehicle and confessing. And he never asked for the right to counsel?" Throughout these exchanges, Ortiz kept his head lowered and his body slanted. After conferring with his attorneys, Ortiz agreed not to pursue the motion to suppress his confession. Deputy Calderon testified that the inventory of the truck was conducted by Ranger Salinas upon Ortiz's apprehension.

September 15, 2018

Ortiz confessed to the killings to his wife and did not request the *Right to Counsel*, according to DA Alaniz. Ranger Salinas conducted the inventory search at a gas station. During a court session at 9:15 a.m., Calderon testified that an AK-47 handgun was discovered in Ortiz's house. However, on March 25, 2024, Ortiz denied ever possessing an AK-47. At 9:17 a.m. during the hearing, Calderon stated that a Prada handbag was found in Ortiz's truck.

The courtroom atmosphere was tense. The Department of Public Safety (DPS) conducted the inventory of the white Dodge truck. Perez's questioning revealed that Captain Calderon was unfamiliar with the inventory process. The truck was discovered at the intersection of Jefferson Street and San Bernardo Avenue; however, no inventory was conducted at that location. The DPS was the sole agency at the scene, with Webb County abstaining from performing the vehicle inventory. Captain Calderon admitted he had not reviewed the policy despite his 17.6 years of experience. He clarified that Ranger Salinas, not Webb County, conducted the vehicle inventory search, and he neither performed the inventory nor obtained a *Search Warrant*.

September 15, 2018

No search was performed initially. The Webb County SWAT team arrested Juan David Ortiz, and his truck was impounded. Ortiz informed Sergeant Noe Gonzalez about the location of the firearm. Ortiz was subsequently charged with multiple homicides, involving victims who were shot in the head.

The video is now playing, capturing the poignant moment when Ortiz was apprehended. In this footage, Ortiz, visibly emotional, is seen weeping. His appearance in the video is noticeably more robust than in previous images.

Under Code Section 32-5-192, concerning implied consent, the procedure for administering tests, and the suspension of driving privileges for refusal to submit to such tests, Ortiz's legal situation becomes clearer. Investigator Noe Gonzalez is sitting next to Ortiz in a vehicle as they transport him following his capture. The handgun, as indicated by Ortiz, was found precisely where he had stated. Importantly, Ortiz was not in the vicinity of the pickup truck, nor was he within reach of the weapon. The Department of Public Safety (DPS) should have secured search warrants, as obtaining a warrant is a necessary prerequisite for arrest.

"Implied consent is not legal," avows Perez.

According to Perez, Ortiz did not give explicit consent for the search of his pickup. However, Calderon argued that implied consent was applicable because Ortiz had corrected the officers regarding the location of the vehicle. Ortiz appears visibly unwell in the video, a state likely attributable to his PTSD. The defense concludes its argument concerning the inventory motion. The prosecution, on the other hand, is expected to summon additional witnesses. Additionally, a questionnaire must be prepared for the jury.

This case is scheduled for trial in San Antonio, Bexar County, on October 21, 2022, at the Bexar County Jury Room. Preliminary hearings will take place in Webb County. Ortiz did not notice my presence and did not glance around during the proceedings.

In July and August, District Attorney Alaniz made the decisive choice not to seek the death penalty against Juan David Ortiz. This decision came after consultations with the families of the victims. DA Alaniz met with the families on two occasions—first on January 25, 2022, and again in July 2022—to discuss this matter extensively in both meetings.

OCTOBER 5, 2022

On October 5, 2022, Webb County District Attorney Isidro Alaniz requested the removal of the death penalty and instead pursued a sentence of life without parole for Juan David Ortiz. This date coincided with Yom Kippur, the Day of Atonement, in Israel, recognized as the most sacred day in the Jewish calendar. Traditionally, Jews seek forgiveness from both God and fellow humans on this day. According to religious beliefs, Yom Kippur is when God determines each individual's fate, thus encouraging repentance and atonement for sins committed during the preceding year.

Yom Kippur represents an annual period of spiritual cleansing for the Temple, the priesthood, and the Jewish community, offering a renewed beginning. On this singular occasion, the High Priest would enter the Holy of Holies. Leviticus 16 details the divinely mandated ceremony performed annually, symbolizing Jesus Christ's future atonement for humanity's sins.

The Western Wall, a revered Jewish prayer site since the Middle Ages, is esteemed for its historical endurance. Many Jews consider the wall sanctified and blessed by God. Each year, the Rabbi receives numerous letters addressed to "God, Jerusalem," which are placed in the wall's crevices. Subsequently, these notes are collected and interred on the Mount of Olives, adhering to ritualistic practices.

A photograph of Juan David Ortiz and a note imploring divine intervention to prevent his execution were placed at the Western Wall in Jerusalem. The challenge was ensuring the note fit securely within one of the wall's fissures.

JD: I called to inform you that I truly believe God spared my life because you left the note at the Western Wall. Do you want to know why I am convinced the wish was fulfilled? On October 5, 2022, Yom Kippur, a significant holiday in Israel, the DA announced the withdrawal of the death penalty pursuit.

Author: I was unaware of Yom Kippur... thank you for informing me. And thank you for believing in me. Many people doubt the reality of God and the sanctity of the Western Wall.

I believe divine intervention through the families and DA Alaniz saved JD's life. God often works through individuals. If God wills him to live, it serves a purpose. It is worth noting that Saint Paul, a former persecutor, authored much of the New Testament. Perhaps God intends for Juan David to minister within the confines of the prison. Life holds a unique purpose for everyone.

The Western Wall entrance in Jerusalem, Israel. *Courtesy of the author*

The Western Wall. *Courtesy of the author*

Leaving note at the Western Wall for Juan David Ortiz. *Courtesy of the author*

The note was left at the Western Wall for Juan David Ortiz. *Courtesy of the author*

CHAPTER 5
TRIAL DIARY

FIRST DAY OF TRIAL

MONDAY

NOVEMBER 28, 2022

Juan David Ortiz appeared in court donned in a black suit and glasses. Positioned in the second row, I observed his mother and uncle in the front row. The case is formidable, heightening the significance of my seating arrangement. I feel privileged to observe these proceedings up close—

During proceedings, cellular communication was prohibited, and photography was restricted, necessitating my phone to remain on silent. Ortiz's mother, characterized by her blonde hair and impeccable nails, exuded a striking presence and elegant appearance.

This occasion marked a rare glimpse of Ortiz in a non-restrained, civilian appearance. This is the closest I will ever be to JD in a composed state—absent of restraints and inmate attire. Ortiz turned to acknowledge his mother and the woman seated beside her, taking in the familial support present in the courtroom.

Ortiz, of slight build and towering stature, with a left-handed stance, was actively taking notes with his legal team. The courtroom staff inquired whether I was a juror or a member of the media. I replied, "No," and they left me undisturbed. I hope JD received the books I sent via Amazon. He previously mentioned to me that his twin sisters were being followed by the media at their university, which seemed to border on harassment. I, too, was taking notes, albeit not on my phone.

The State was represented by seven staff members, while Ortiz had only two. JD later confided in me:

JD: "I'm allowed to have up to three defense attorneys, but Joel Perez, my attorney, never pursued getting a third attorney approved in my case. I wanted to retain Joey Tellez. He made efforts to communicate with me, even sending his female staff to visit me at the jail. Perez, on the other hand, never visited me or communicated with me. He was preoccupied with his campaign and neglected my case."

Author: "I regret that Eddie Peña wasn't your defense attorney. He would have diligently handled your case and provided transparent counsel. In Laredo, he's the sole certified capital murder defense attorney. For capital murder cases here, lawyers from San Antonio and Austin are summoned when Eddie Peña is occupied. Joey Tellez wasn't certified for capital murder defense, which prevented him from remaining on your legal team. Consider if you were innocent; the odds would have been stacked against you."

Meanwhile, JD's mother, engrossed in a book, mirrors his penchant for reading voraciously. I noticed Laredo Media personnel seated nearby, having parked their vehicle in the same lot as mine. As the jury entered, a wave of apprehension swept over me—it's daunting to think they hold Juan David's fate in their hands.

The State of Texas vs. Juan David Ortiz

This trial is about to become profoundly significant. I am here to meticulously document the proceedings. Ortiz adamantly pled NOT GUILTY, and District Attorney Alaniz began distributing evidence to the jury, who maintained solemn expressions. DA Alaniz depicted Erika Peña as a heroic figure to the jury.

DA Alaniz: "Handsome, kind, and tall... Erika Peña had been with him four to five times before. At 204 Bur Oak Drive, Juan David Ortiz's wife was in San Antonio, Texas, attending the Canelo fight. He was fearful; Melissa had his DNA because he was the last one with her."

Alaniz underscored that the jury would see Juan David Ortiz's confession, alongside evidence including the murder weapon, casings, forensic analysis, expert testimonies, and video footage.

Continuing, Alaniz emphasized the gravity of the case: "This is about a man who betrayed his badge, his country, his family, and his community." The victims were tragically killed execution-style, their families left in tears. Ortiz entered establishments casually, purchasing cold beer, seemingly unfazed.

"Erika knew him for five months," Alaniz elucidated further. "He provided for her, buying food and drugs. She saw him as a good person, unaware of his role as a Border Patrol Supervisor. She even knew where he lived."

Despite Ortiz's position of authority, Alaniz highlighted that he conducted law enforcement duties with apparent dignity and respect.

Ortiz left his weapon in the truck during the incident.

3:28 a.m.

Miranda Warning on September 15, 2018

Perez: "Focus on Ortiz's demeanor, his hand movements, and facial expressions. He experienced blackouts, is an Iraq war veteran, and takes medication for anxiety, depression, and PTSD prescribed by the VA. Ortiz admitted to knowing Erika and pointing a gun at her but claimed he had no intention to harm her."

Perez: "He is a law-abiding citizen who served his country, is a family man, and is a good man."

The jury's expressions remained profoundly serious.

Perez spoke softly: "The burden is to prove beyond a reasonable doubt. Erika Peña uses $300 to $400 daily on crack and heroin. No inventory search was conducted on JD's truck."

DA Alaniz: "Objection."

Perez: "They began reading Ortiz his rights only after placing him in a controlled room. He was read his rights in a controlled environment. He is a war veteran who was suicidal, experiencing blackouts, and under the influence of psychotropic medications. His confession, given 9 to 11 hours later, was coerced with promises to his wife, with the DA present. There is no definitive evidence that he is the triggerman. This is a case of a false confession involving a war veteran. Ortiz was not in the National Crime Information Center."

Testimony of Erika Peña

Erika Peña is the subsequent witness to take the stand.

Perez: He was an Intelligence Federal Officer, while they were State Officers.

Erika Peña, of a heavier build with blonde hair, appeared fully covered in clothing as she directed her gaze towards Juan David Ortiz. Presently 31 years old, Peña was born and raised in Laredo and is unmarried. She has a 12-year-old child and possesses a criminal record with over a dozen offenses. She maintained direct eye contact as she testified, having recently completed a two-year probationary period.

District Attorney Alaniz read the charges against her. Peña, not addicted, has been on methadone for a year and was incarcerated for five to six months, with her probation revoked for failure to report. Her legal troubles began at 21 and have been intermittent since then.

Joel Perez employed his status as a war veteran with PTSD as a defense strategy to the jury.

Peña disclosed that she engaged in escorting, providing sexual services for money. Initially claiming to have started this work at 23, she later admitted to beginning at 17.

As she looked at Ortiz, she recounted, "David was a friend. He was a client the first time."

David averted his gaze. Peña added, "I guess you could say that about being a client."

She testified that David had once damaged her phone and noted that she was residing in a hotel at the time. Despite her testimony, Peña appeared unafraid of David, frequently looking at him when discussing her fear. David had picked her up in his white Dodge truck numerous times, though she could not specify how often.

He would call her, and their encounters were sporadic. She first met him a block away from the Evelyn Hotel on Jefferson Street. Peña recounted to the jury that she had sexual relations with him but could not recall the frequency. She described David as genuinely nice, sweet, and funny. He would drop her off at her office on San Bernardo Ave after their encounters. She did not observe any signs of depression, suicidal tendencies, anxiety, or odd behavior in David. They had visited the Cactus Motel once and frequently parked on random streets to engage in sexual activities.

Peña affirmed that David did not use drugs, although he was aware of her preference. He would provide her with money but did not purchase substances for her as she had previously stated. They did not engage in sexual relations at the Evelyn Hotel. Peña identified her pink flowered bag and mentioned that she had bought him Bud Light Tall Boys. She remained composed and undaunted of David. She admitted to visiting his house and was familiar with his residence. Peña identified a receipt for Bud Light and Powerade, noting that David had given her a $100 bill.

Although she does not own a vehicle, she knows how to drive. Peña recounted sitting at the corner of the table, near the kitchen, when David's family was out of town in McAllen, Texas. She was dissolving heroin and injecting it when David came out with mouthwash for her and instructed her to shower. They did not engage in sexual activity that afternoon. Peña noted David's anxiety and uncharacteristic behavior upon his arrival. She was shaking as she grabbed the cigarettes and felt scared, leading her to sit in a chair without a phone. Peña went outside, felt nauseous, and vomited. She continued to look at David in court.

"The DA was leading," said Perez.

Erika Peña grapples with her disclosure. She recounts the sequence: David was the penultimate person to engage in sexual intercourse with Melissa. Erika Peña surmised David as Melissa's potential assailant due to his apparent fearlessness. Erika, having abstained from eating all day, speculates David secured the house entrance. Her initial intention upon arriving was sexual engagement, though specifics evade her memory—estimating fewer than five instances, encompassing oral sex and foreplay. David bore two distinctive tattoos of hummingbirds. Erika identified these markings in photographs, alongside an American flag. Their casual outing for a burger concluded behind a trailer, where David brandished a firearm. Erika recalled feeling apprehensive, met with David's silence when queried about returning her to her initial location. Without response, he wielded the gun in his left hand, aiming it directly at her countenance while seizing her with his right hand. Her subsequent actions involved disrobing and fleeing the vehicle, seeking assistance from a State Trooper, detailing an encounter where she faced a firearm threat..

Erika Peña cannot recall the specific street now, but she could at the time. She identified Ortiz's residence. In court, she frequently gazes at him. Unaware of his law enforcement affiliation, Erika accompanied Ortiz to *Old Score* for drug transactions. Ortiz maintained romantic relationships with both Erika and Melissa concurrently. Erika recognized Ortiz picking up Melissa, who had a longer-standing relationship with him than Erika, spanning several years. Devastatingly, all the victims in the photographs were her friends. She encountered Melissa in jail. Janelle, her closest friend, was recalled fondly by Erika during District Attorney Alaniz's attempt to humanize her through anecdotes of Janelle's humor. Melissa, who Erika found to be humorous and capable of brightening any room, left her family in tears from the front row of the courtroom. Erika was at the police station during Ortiz's apprehension. He did not solicit sex workers during work hours in a government vehicle.

Erika complimented Ortiz's house, although she did not recall seeing any family photos. Ortiz had previously taken her to his residence twice.

She affirmed that she did not engage in showering, sexual activities, or oral sex with him at his residence. Erika admitted to engaging in sexual activities either in a parking lot, behind Walmart, in or behind a hotel, or in a hotel room, though she could not recollect the number of times she had been taken by Ortiz to purchase drugs from *Old Score*.

Ortiz, observing his mother, appeared extremely thin with his pants slipping down; his oversized suit added to his disheveled appearance.

Erika Peña's 2019 rehabilitation attempt proved unsuccessful, as she continues to rely on methadone. Joel Perez queried why she persists with methadone, to which she responded, having previously used heroin followed by crack, that she remains alert under its influence. Erika is under the effects of methadone—on methadone right now. It's a—synthetic heroin. She acknowledged hearing a voice during her previous interaction with the trooper, attributing it to her deceased ex-boyfriend, emphasizing her high state at the time.

Ortiz diligently documented notes throughout the proceedings.

She expressed frustration during her testimony, vehemently asserting her sanity under oath.

Erika is under oath and said Ortiz pointed to her chest—now she is pointing to her head this time.

A red-haired juror adopted a notably solemn expression while observing Joel Perez and Ortiz.

Drugs affected her memory. Erika Peña assaulted a peace officer and can't remember doing this. She has PTSD, anxiety, and severe depression. Erika Peña stated that David said to her, "What's the word?"

At one point, she worked as a housekeeper at Hotel Marriott, but presently, she does not. She has housing—and is seeing someone who is helping her pay.

State Trooper Francisco Martinez described her as visibly frightened, dressed in a bra and white pants.

Ortiz, seemingly scanned the courtroom. He was not handcuffed and gazed at the nearby sheriff and his firearm.

Erika was wearing a red bra and white pants. She can't breathe.

D.O. sought clarification from Erika Peña regarding Ortiz's appearance, described as "guero, alto, beige shirt" (translation: blonde, tall, beige shirt). "Alguien no está ahí" (translation: Nobody is there) was her assertion about Ortiz's residence.

The jury temporarily exited as the DPS video was screened. Erika recalled meeting Ortiz on four to five occasions. According to her, he had separated from his wife.

"La casa estaba sola." Translation: The house was alone, said Erika.

"Erika affirmed that the house was empty," indicating Ortiz's intention to bring her to his room, dressed in a beige shirt, slim pants, and work boots. Ortiz, a supervisor somewhere, became the subject of her police report. She was visibly shocked.

"You can solve the case if you think about it. These women were murdered at night; you never know?" DPS Francisco told Erika Peña. He obscured the camera.

"Alguien tiene que hablar por ellas," translated as "Someone has to speak for them," DPS Francisco informed Erika Peña.

The DPS Trooper's decision to obscure the camera in the footage stemmed from his desire to prevent his interaction with her from being recorded. Subsequently, he again obscured the camera to communicate privately with her, an action perceived as unconventional.

Erika recounted, "Me quiso agarrar completamente," meaning "He wanted to grab me completely." Additionally, Erika Peña mentioned to the trooper that Ortiz possessed a black, robust firearm.

Law enforcement officials visited Ortiz's home, which is a five-minute drive from Sand Hill Street, where he resides. The incident involving her and Ortiz occurred near Loop 20 and McPherson, towards Border Patrol (Circle K), where he brandished a firearm from his white Dodge truck. She fled to a state trooper for safety.

The DPS trooper again covers the camera. Erika requests cigarettes. Trooper Francisco Hernandez is identified as the DPS trooper.

Jurors are unable to retain translations of the video. Exhibit 15 is currently being played. Exhibit 16 features the State Trooper within the exhibit. State exhibits 17 depict Erika Peña with the State Trooper. A man taking pictures of a white Mustang is shown in this exhibit. Erika Peña went to the store; the State Trooper was not present.

DA Alaniz references case law provided by the ADA during court proceedings. The proceedings were aired on Court TV. The incident occurred west of Circle K, Loop 20, and McPherson, at the gas station. The jury is currently viewing footage of Erika Peña with DPS. Jurors are reviewing transcripts. I observe their facial expressions and demeanors. All jurors are using tablets and transcripts to follow the proceedings.

"El vato va La San Ber," stated Erika Peña, indicating the individual in question goes to San Bernardo Ave.

"Sand Hill Street is where David lives," Peña added. Subsequently, the trooper contacted Ranger Salinas.

Erika recounted, "Que la casa estaba sola." Translation: "The house was alone.

"Siempre me gustaba pero lo tiraba a león, porque él se iba con Melissa," Erika continued. Translation: "I always liked him, but I would blow him off because he would leave with Melissa."

"Él era bien necio." Translation: "He was very stubborn," Erika noted.

"Melissa no era mi amiga; la vi en el condado." Translation: "Melissa was not my friend; I saw her in the county jail," Erika stated.

The Department of Public Safety did not *Mirandize* Juan David Ortiz.

TUESDAY

DAY 2 OF THE TRIAL

NOVEMBER 29, 2022

Commenced at 8:15 a.m.

The court session began with the viewing of a video depicting a white truck pulling into a gas station. Trooper Bradshaw was called to testify, detailing the moment when Ortiz was seen fleeing the scene. Notably, an 18-wheeler obliterated the camera worn by the Department of Public Safety (DPS) officer.

District Attorney Alaniz utilized satellite technology to establish the location. Ortiz's mother and his young twin sister were present. During his testimony, Trooper Bradshaw maintained a robotic demeanor. The video showed State Trooper Javier Obregon, while Bradshaw instructed, "Turn around, hands up." Ortiz exhibited signs of nervousness and questioned, "How does the truck match the murder?" Subsequently, Ortiz fled on foot.

Trooper Bradshaw explained his process for linking Ortiz's truck to the murders. He struggled for breath as he pursued Ortiz in the video. Multiple law enforcement agencies, including the Texas Rangers, Webb County Sheriff's Office, and State Troopers, arrived at the scene. The commanding officer shouted, "David Ortiz, come out!"

It took approximately 2 to 2.6 hours to secure and contain the area. Lead investigators Fred Calderon and EJ Salinas were on-site at the Ava Hotel. The prosecution entered a black truck, parked in space #22, as evidence. This vehicle was where Ortiz was found hiding.

Joel Perez testified that Ortiz did not abandon his truck. The Webb County authorities took custody of Ortiz.

Trooper Bradshaw testified that he did not observe any activity suggesting the vehicle was being towed. Ortiz admitted ownership of the vehicle, stating, "Yeah, this is my vehicle."

Trooper Obregon took the stand, and exhibits #22 and #23 were submitted. Obregon was observed examining Ortiz's vehicle in the video, emphasizing his role. He was unaware that Ortiz was targeting individuals. Trooper Bradshaw first made contact with Ortiz, followed by Obregon, who found Ortiz armed only with a handgun.

Ortiz, identified as a suspect in two murders, was recorded saying, "You are freaking me out."

Joel Perez argued that the State Trooper was not legally qualified to determine if Ortiz had abandoned his vehicle.

Ortiz's twin sister, who displayed kindness by offering water outside the courtroom, attended the trial. Mr. Wood mentioned the potential testimony of Dr. Stern. Trooper Obregon described Ortiz as confused and evading arrest. His body camera footage showed him placing handcuffs on Ortiz and inquiring about any weapons. Ortiz claimed he had no weapon on his person, stating it was in his truck. They conducted a search and found no weapons on Ortiz, who remarked, "You already know my name." Obregon retrieved a lighter and a set of keys from Ortiz's pockets but did not search his truck, which was no longer present. Obregon's demeanor appeared genuine.

Noe Hernandez, affiliated with the Webb County District Attorney's Office, Sheriff's Office, and a SWAT member with four years of military service in Afghanistan, testified. Exhibits #24 to #32 were presented to Hernandez. Ortiz was observed taking notes. Hernandez confirmed his presence at the crime scene after Ortiz's confession and watching the interview, though not in person. Exhibit #33, featuring a vehicle with a Disabled Vet license plate belonging to Ortiz, was admitted into evidence.

Law enforcement officials, including DPS and Webb County sheriffs, deemed Ortiz armed and dangerous due to his crimes. The jury viewed the truck where Ortiz was found lying down. Hernandez grabbed Ortiz's arm while Ortiz was facing up, and Ortiz did not resist.

Felix Nunez searched the vehicle for Ortiz's weapon.

Keys, a phone, and cigarettes were found on Ortiz. He was placed in second-hand cuffs to aid his breathing. Ortiz had trouble breathing, and they removed his boots, finding no injuries. Ortiz was taken into custody without being Mirandized. The transport was video-recorded. Evidence #35 was submitted.

Ortiz, who had been suicidal, stated, "Take your trophy shot. I took my pain meds."

The Assistant District Attorney attempted to compare Ortiz's PTSD to Noe Hernandez's Afghanistan tour, asking, "You went to war. And did you kill when you got back?" Perez objected to this line of questioning.

Ortiz was hyperventilating and was double handcuffed. He did not speak during this time. Hernandez, who had been awake for 48 hours, testified about finding the last victim face down at Mile 13, on the outskirts of town. The court recessed until 1:15 p.m.

Hernandez stated that Felix Nunez did not allow him to Mirandize Ortiz. Evidence collected would have been handed over to Calderon or Nunez. They never returned to Ortiz's truck for a property inventory. Ortiz shook his head in disagreement with the witness's statement about the inventory list. Robert Castillo presented evidence, including a gun, a tire, and an envelope. The envelope contained items that matched the casings. The State labeled the projectiles as evidence.

Officer Stern, a new property officer with only three weeks on the job, testified. Fred Calderon, the lead investigator, also testified. They received a 911 call reporting a lifeless body, marking the first of four murders. The first victim, Melissa Ramirez, was found shortly after noon, with two shell casings discovered at the scene. The second day, another shell casing was found. Ramirez was wearing white shorts and no shoes, lying face down, clutching M&M's, and had trauma to the back of her head.

Ortiz's motive remains a critical question. Joel Perez helped Ortiz with his suit in a touching moment, highlighting the bond between the lawyer and client. Ortiz left for a break, appearing ill during the trial. He was observed making an "L" shape on his leg with his fingers, a habitual gesture.

Calderon detailed the evidence from the crime scenes:

Scene #1: Discovery of the Incident

A .40 caliber Federal-type firearm was discovered at the scene. Calderon observed two .40 caliber casings situated a few feet from the body of a woman.

Scene #2: Evidence of the Crime

At the scene, a .40 caliber shell casing was located a few feet from the woman's body, accompanied by traces of blood.

Scene #3: Witness Testimony

Calderon testified that he witnessed two .40 caliber shell casings at the scene.

Scene #4: Additional Forensic Evidence

Forensic analysis of the scene revealed several crucial pieces of evidence: a small quantity ball of crack cocaine, distinct tire tracks in close proximity to the woman, a damaged casket, and two sets of tire tracks.

September 13

Additional Investigation Details:

On September 13, forensic analysis confirmed that the second .40 caliber casing matched the firearm found at the scene. Calderon, a seasoned investigator with 13 years of experience, played a crucial role in the investigation.

Judge Hale stated that it is at the discretion of the media to decide whether to publicize images of the murder. Melissa Ramirez was identified through fingerprints as she had no ID or cell phone. A 911 call reported her body, and a pickup truck was seen near the scene, but no probable cause was found to arrest Ortiz initially. Dr. Stern conducted the preliminary examination, and Ortiz was not initially a suspect. The second murder appeared to be an auto-pedestrian accident but was later linked to Ortiz.

Claudine Luera, seen with Ramirez, was found a couple of miles from the first murder scene on September 14. Erika Peña's testimony was pivotal, as her escape led to Ortiz's capture. She described Ortiz's large oil field truck and identified Ortiz as her assailant at 204 Bur Oak Drive, Laredo, Texas. Peña testified that she had been hired by Ortiz for sex multiple times. Federico Calderon had the vehicle towed, consolidating the evidence against Ortiz.

The second homicide initially appeared to be a case of auto-pedestrian incident, yet evidence proved otherwise. Several miles from Melissa Ramirez's murder site, Claudine Luera was found. Luera had recently been in contact with Ramirez. At 9:00 p.m. on September 14, a trooper arrived with Erika Peña to query with Calderon. Had Erika Peña not escaped, Ortiz might have eluded capture.

Ortiz possessed unusually elongated and gaunt hands, having noticeably shed significant weight. Erika Peña exhibited profound fear. She recounted Ortiz owning a large oil field truck. She explicitly accused David of assaulting her at his residence located at 204 Bur Oak Drive, Laredo, Texas 78045. Erika stated that Ortiz had paid her for sexual services multiple times as a common thing, contradicting her previous testimony where she claimed to have been with David on four to five occasions. Federico Calderon had the vehicle towed away.

WEDNESDAY

DAY 3 OF THE TRIAL

11:30 a.m.

NOVEMBER 30, 2022

During the interrogation video, Ortiz is disclosing his confession to Calderon. Ortiz denied having knowledge of the photographs depicting the two purses. In court, Ortiz observed my presence. Upon arrival, I positioned myself behind his mother.

Erika Peña previously indicated that Ortiz wore a tan or beige shirt paired with light trousers. In the confession room video, Ortiz is observed fidgeting with his hair. Subsequent to 3:00 a.m. in the confession footage, Calderon emerged, announcing the discovery of weapons.

Officers initially refrained from entering Ortiz's residence during their initial visit with Erika Peña due to the absence of a search warrant. Subsequent to Ortiz's arrest, a warrant was secured, prompting law enforcement to enter his residence between approximately 1:00 p.m. and 2:00 p.m., subsequent to his confession. Ortiz expressed reluctance for law enforcement to disturb his residence. Upon their entry, authorities discovered an array of weaponry. Following Erika's escape, Ortiz returned home, retrieved his weapons, but departed prior to the arrival of law enforcement, subsequently perpetrating the homicides of two additional women, Guíselda and Janelle. Interrogators queried Ortiz about the firearm found in his vehicle, specifically noting its utilization of .40 caliber government-issued ammunition. During his confession, Ortiz exhibited self-satisfied behavior, including solitary clapping and smiling. Ortiz informed a trooper of his physical condition, asserting he outpaced the trooper. Throughout the confession proceedings, numerous officers repeatedly observed Ortiz in the interrogation room. Ranger Salinas inquired about Ortiz's susceptibility to blackouts, with Ortiz periodically appearing somnolent during the video. E.J. Salinas and Fred Calderon subsequently entered the room, closed the door, and removed Ortiz's handcuffs.

3:21 a.m.

Saturday

September 20, 2018

Daniella Ortiz (Juan David Ortiz's spouse) was driving a truck in San Antonio with her three children. An AR15 firearm was positioned on the kitchen counter. Simultaneously, Daniella was en route to Laredo, Texas, where she intended to engage in discussions with Juan David (JD). Ortiz professed the presence of a thriving marital relationship while situated in San Antonio (SA). His relocation to Laredo was motivated by a career advancement opportunity.

Ortiz disclosed, "I was prescribed Paxil for my PTSD and anxiety, along with Trazodone for sleep. Additionally, I suffer from high blood pressure and anger issues."

Ortiz expressed frustration with the Veterans Affairs (VA), stating, "The VA fucked up ... I have no criminal record."

Ortiz visited the Veterans Affairs (VA) facility in Laredo for treatment. He consulted Dr. Shankar, a psychiatrist, specifically for his sleep issues. As part of his treatment regimen, Ortiz underwent a 12-week therapy program with Patricia Amparan.

Ortiz recounted, "I was doing fine until I started going to the VA."

He acknowledged his suicidal thoughts, confessing, "I couldn't admit it because of my role as a law enforcement supervisor."

Regarding his medication, Ortiz stated, "The VA increased my dosage."

Reflecting on his personal life, Ortiz lamented, "I had a great marriage."

Professionally, he declared, "I was very proficient in my work."

Ortiz recalled his VA visit in February and admitted to consuming alcohol alongside his medication. He detailed numerous appointments with VA doctors, totaling 40 in number. Ortiz self-proclaimed to occasionally taking pills and struggling with anger issues. He mentioned undergoing periodic background checks, which occur every five years. Ortiz's wife traveled to visit her sister, to see the Canelo fight, in San Antonio during which a household leak expedited her departure. Ortiz advised her to keep their children in San Antonio.

Ortiz denied involvement with a pink purse. He stated, "You all have the keys, so take what you want."

Planning an early departure to San Antonio, Ortiz explained, "I was going to drive in the morning to meet up with my wife and family."

He acknowledged consuming five pills and subsequently blacking out. Ortiz disclosed his familiarity with an AR15 rifle used for hunting and his past rental of a ranch. He claimed his wife was unaware of his actions, particularly his extensive drinking habits.

Ortiz admitted, "My drinking is a significant issue; I started smoking. I didn't have a hangover."

He mentioned picking up Tall Boys in front of Walmart and ignoring calls from Gabby Nunez. Ortiz told Nunez to advise his wife not to drive to Laredo.

Ortiz admitted, "I was waiting to be shot in the back of the truck. The troopers knew I wasn't armed—that's why they didn't shoot."

He expressed familiarity with evasive tactics learned from his law enforcement career, stating, "Never stop running and you won't get caught."

Ortiz identified his workplace as Laredo North Station, under the supervision of Juan C. Rivera.

Regarding his work, Ortiz emphasized the meticulous nature of his duties, stating, " I put in detail. You have to study the hours."

He acknowledged Rick Benavides as a supervisor and expressed aspirations for a promotion to the second floor.

Ortiz claimed ignorance about blood stains on his boots, insisting, "I had no idea."

Ortiz's blackout episodes are linked to alcohol and medication consumption. Ortiz recalled experiencing nightmares and verbally lashing out during blackout episodes. "I have nightmares and say 'fuck you' in my blackouts," said Ortiz. He admitted his wife would slap him awake during these episodes. Ortiz recounted a story from his military service in Iraq, expressing memory loss upon returning home. He mentioned his wife's observation that Trazodone was insufficient for his insomnia. The author interjected, sharing personal experience with Trazodone, stating, "I took Trazodone, and it didn't alleviate my insomnia."

Calderon pointed out, "Ortiz has blood on his boot, not from animals."

Ortiz responded with resignation, "If what you're saying is true, I'm fucked."

Calderon dismissed certain individuals, remarking, "Those people—"

Ortiz expressed despair, stating, "There is no help for me if what you are saying is true."

Calderon commented, "Those people won't be missed."

Ortiz disclosed his cell number, "(956) 455-3233."

Calderon noted, "They aren't productive members of society."

Ortiz mentioned his wife's role as a homemaker and affirmed his recollection of events on a Thursday.

He vehemently denied engaging with prostitutes, asserting, "I don't fuck prostitutes! I was a Doc Medic; the last thing I would do is fuck a prostitute."

The possibility of Juan David (Ortiz) suffering from Traumatic Brain Injury (TBI) is a significant concern. One might ponder the underlying causes of his blackouts and whether these episodes are amenable to treatment.

During his time in the confession room, Ortiz experienced a sudden collapse. He appeared heavily sedated, exhibiting peculiar and erratic behaviors, including consuming chips and water. His conduct was noticeably awkward. In the waiting room, he oscillated between falling asleep with his head down and intermittently eating Doritos when left unaccompanied.

At one point, Ortiz queried a Sheriff's Deputy about his morning workout routine. Calderon reassured Ortiz that assistance was available to him, provided he remained alive and was not buried six feet under. Ortiz then inquired if many people at Sally Port smoked, directing this question to an officer stationed outside the confession door.

Throughout the confession video, Ortiz was observed fiddling with the chair.

Calderon confronted Ortiz, stating, "I know that you feel that these people shouldn't be here. They are not productive in society."

Ortiz responded emphatically, asserting, "Nobody drives my truck but me," and added that his wife was responsible for dropping off their child at pre-K.

5:38 a.m.

The blood discovered on Ortiz's boot was subjected to forensic analysis but did not yield any leads. Gunshot Residue (GSR) testing, which is instrumental in detecting gunpowder, was notably absent from the investigative procedures.

DAY 4 OF THE TRIAL

THURSDAY

DECEMBER 1, 2022

8:30 a.m.

Ortiz: When I panic ... I get on my pills.

Calderon: All the victims were HIV positive and had Hepatitis C. I'm concerned about your wife. Tell your wife to get checked.

Ortiz: She is good to go.

Ortiz: Everything is under my name. It won't affect my wife's credit.

Calderon informs Ortiz of the discovery of crack pipes and needles in his vehicle and residence.

Ortiz: I got myself checked, and I'm clean.

Ortiz dampens his hair with water in the confession video, subsequently breaking down in tears within the interrogation room.

Author: Witnessing his emotional display was poignant. Despite his transgressions, Ortiz displays genuine humanity and remorse.

September 15, 2018

Ortiz consented to DNA sampling at 10:45 a.m. on September 15, 2018. He was instructed to sign for the DNA sample, which he administered himself (DNA swab).

Ortiz requested a printed family photograph from his phone to commence dialogue—a Mother's Day image with a call to his spouse—ultimately agreeing to the arrangement.

Federico Calderon and E.J. Salinas coerced Ortiz into donning a prison uniform, seizing his attire as evidentiary artifacts. Subsequently, they instructed him to divest himself of his undergarments, precipitating his stark metamorphosis from a commendable citizen, distinguished war veteran, and productive member of society into the confines of a prisoner.

During this turbulent episode, Calderon directed Ortiz's wife to return to San Antonio, procuring a photograph of Ortiz's family thereafter. In an endeavor to engender cooperation, Calderon purportedly interceded with District Attorney Alaniz, advocating on Ortiz's behalf.

In a moment immortalized on the confession recording, Ortiz succumbed to tears, seemingly grasping the irreversible nature of his errors and the profound repercussions on his life. This instance underscores the premise that a solitary, ill-fated decision possesses the capacity to irreversibly reshape one's existence. The course of life, thus, hinges on the decisions we elect to make, each choice serving as a pivotal juncture that determines our fate.

Despite Calderon's pledges to intercede with the District Attorney, the prosecution maintained steadfast resolve in seeking the death penalty for Ortiz. It became apparent that Calderon's professed support was a calculated maneuver intended to elicit a confession from Ortiz.

In summation, this narrative underscores the intricate interplay between justice and stratagem in the pursuit of truth within the realm of criminal investigations.

Ortiz expressed, "I am the pride and joy of the family." He also remarked, "My mother is going to have a heart attack." Witnessing the confession in court, Ortiz's mother broke down in tears upon hearing these words. One can empathize with her profound anguish; presumably, she devoted herself tirelessly to raising Ortiz as a single mother. At the age of 17, she enlisted Ortiz in the Navy, believing her parental duties were fulfilled, only to have her heart shattered by his actions. Regardless of their children's choices, parents invariably harbor an enduring love. Nonetheless, exceptions exist, as evidenced by parents who forsake their offspring, disavowing any connection.

Ortiz admitted Erika had been at his residence. He acknowledged consorting with prostitutes, stating, "Melissa only gave me a BJ (blow job)."

He disclosed, "I became aware that Erika had reported me near Winchester and Monarch, prompting my flight."

Ortiz confessed and furnished details concerning Janelle.

The author reflected, "The pivotal moment ... the confession. Ortiz is culpable. Why then assert 'Not Guilty'?" The author pondered.

Ortiz remarked, "Anna Gabriella—I picked her up one time. She would call me."

Ortiz transported the sex workers to the crack house and subsequently reported that location.

Ortiz recounted, "Melissa was a friend ... San Ber (San Bernardo) friend. I would ALWAYS go with Erika to the crack house," as expressed in his own words.

DAY 5 OF THE TRIAL

FRIDAY

DECEMBER 2, 2022

The following transcript is verbatim from court testimony:

Ortiz was unaware he was being recorded in the interrogation room. He persistently shook his head in denial, asserting he was oblivious to the presence of a camera in the room, an action Calderon purportedly orchestrated intentionally.

By 11:30 a.m., the confession had concluded within the courtroom, where Ortiz's mother and uncle, visibly distressed, were witnessed weeping in the elevator post-viewing. When asked of their well-being, Ortiz's uncle, struggling to compose himself, managed to affirm their condition. Witnessing their emotional turmoil in response to Ortiz's confession was deeply poignant—a stark illustration of their unexpected shock and heartbreak. Ortiz's actions, engaging in illicit acts with prostitutes and resulting in their deaths, inflicted profound anguish upon his family. Could one reproach them? Who among us would wish to witness such transgressions from a son raised under strict moral guidance?

Ortiz's response was a terse "No," declining to provide his version of events. Calderon disregarded Ortiz's refusal, thereby infringing upon his rights, Ranger Salinas neglected to inquire if Ortiz intended to waive those rights.

Ortiz, who served eight years in military duty and consumed eight pills daily, remarked, "From the day I was born, I was a squared away bastard," expressing remorse at his perceived failure in both personal and military contexts. He recalled getting blackouts. Ortiz disclosed mixing Tall Boys (beer) with medications.

"I am a disgrace to myself and the military," Ortiz confessed.

Ortiz disclosed being prescribed seizure medication. Ortiz, a former Navy corpsman, recounted witnessing harrowing scenes during his deployment, experiences that left lasting psychological scars.

He disclosed suicidal ideation, lamenting, "If I had my gun, I would have shot myself." Ortiz revealed never having met his father and having attempted suicide.

Ortiz desired solitary confinement, seeking a separate cell within the prison. He offered to provide a confession in exchange for this condition.

"I need my medication," Ortiz beseeched, a plea Calderon denied.

Joel Perez: The term "if" serves as a conditional clause within the discourse of District Attorney Alaniz, the individual who holds the decisive power over Ortiz's fate. Calderon engaged in a dialogue with District Attorney Alaniz during a confession. Notably, Calderon neglected to document his conversation with Alaniz. The ultimate decision rests with District Attorney Alaniz, embodying a scenario of quid pro quo, with Ortiz as the captive audience. Ortiz initially resisted the interview. He discusses his impending retirement and his desire for his wife to retain his pension.

As I descended to the lower floor, I observed a juror entering the elevator. Choosing to forgo the ride, I informed the juror, "I cannot join you; you are on the jury."

In the interrogation video, Ortiz emphatically replied, "Fucking no," when asked if he wanted to make a statement.

E.J. Salinas served as the documentarian for this case. DA Alaniz proclaimed during the confession that Ortiz claimed there were no occurrences of blackouts; he characterized all such claims as falsehoods.

Erika Peña was present at the station simultaneously with Ortiz. District Attorney Alaniz spoke loudly in court. According to Ortiz, he fervently maintained that he was never offered an attorney. District Attorney Alaniz stated, "Since Ortiz was a law enforcement officer, he should know his rights—and he never asked for an attorney."

Calderon averred that preservation photographs were taken, and the truck was subsequently towed to the Sheriff's Office for a thorough search. In the context of vehicle security, a "fob" refers to a device that remotely unlocks and locks a vehicle. A fob facilitates access to a truck by enabling remote opening. Ortiz's truck, however, did not possess such a fob. Calderon remained unaware of this fact regarding the truck's lack of a fob when questioned by Joel Perez.

MONDAY

8:30 a.m.

DECEMBER 5, 2022

2ND WEEK OF TRIAL

Dr. Stern testified in court, providing a detailed pathological diagnosis of Melissa Ramirez's body. This included an identifying photograph of the lower jaw (mandible on the right side), as well as a separate photo displaying a gunshot wound on the cheek, two gunshot wounds on the neck, and one gunshot wound on the right cheek, documented at 12:00 p.m.

A juror fell asleep during the trial, drawing comparisons to Biden's recent dozing incident in Hawaii. The juror, clad in a black shirt, was later replaced by a chubby woman wearing glasses. Media outlets sensationalized the event, falsely suggesting he had fainted upon seeing autopsy photos.

The juror's drowsiness stemmed from a lack of sleep the previous night, as confirmed by the judge's remarks in court. Dr. Stern examined the juror and affirmed his good health. Personally witnessing the incident, I observed the juror close his eyes and slump in his seat, though he did not lose consciousness. Fainting, I noted, involves falling to the floor directly.

The juror was merely dozing off when he leaned on his hand, occasionally nodding forward until he slipped from his seat, causing a commotion in the courtroom.

Next to me, a national media reporter claimed the juror fainted upon viewing the photos, which I dismissed as exaggerated sensationalism aimed at boosting ratings.

In a "serial killer" trial, what garners more attention: reality or spectacle?

The jury, now composed of thirteen members, included only four men and nine women.

"You realize all the victims were women, correct?"

Today, the court proceedings focused on the autopsy reports and their results. The prosecution presented photographs of the bodies.

During a break, Ortiz's mother was seen conversing and interacting with the families of Janelle Ortiz and Guiselda Hernandez outside the courtroom.

Dialogue: JD and the Author

JD: I was praying—inside—in silence ... during my trial.

JD: Let me tell you ... wait ... let me tell you; I saw you ... I saw you outside the court, walking on the sidewalk, when they were driving me back to the jail. You were on your phone with someone; I don't know with whom. But I saw you on the phone with someone. You were on a big phone ... it was a big phone. What I liked about the trial was that I was able to see the outside and the free world; I was able to see freedom through the window ... at least for a little bit. I was in a black SUV.

Author: I remember seeing that black SUV. But I didn't know it was you inside or you that they were driving ... I thought it was a politician or somebody famous they were guarding and protecting; I thought it was the FBI or Secret Service. I remember watching that SUV pass by and getting a weird feeling ... like ... who is in there? And it was you. Out of all the people, you saw me ... LOL!

CONTINUING DECEMBER 5, 2022

During the presentation of the autopsy photographs, family members began to weep, with some opting to step outside to grieve privately. The autopsies revealed that all the gunshot wounds were located in the victims' necks and heads, and each victim tested positive for heroin. Among the victims, either Griselda or Luera exhibited signs of blunt force trauma, though the specific instrument responsible could not be identified, and there was no discernible pattern to the injuries.

Ranger E.J. Salinas, who had been employed by the Department of Public Safety (DPS) and had served at the Sheriff's Office for four and a half years, found connections that suggested a broader conspiracy. The Intelligence Center, a vital resource for all law enforcement agencies, facilitated Salinas's analytical research. The Border Patrol provided federal intelligence, while the state intelligence was also represented, with both entities co-located in the same room upstairs. Two intelligence centers, situated on the same floor, operated daily to share critical information.

Salinas conducted an investigation involving 60 individuals, during which Ortiz, a colleague, worked in the same office. The layout of the office allowed for easy eavesdropping on conversations. Ortiz, making an unpleasant expression, directed his disdain at Ranger Salinas while Salinas recited Ortiz's confession, which revealed Ortiz's access to the database used for running license plates. "The name Jose Dominguez Hernandez led me here," stated Salinas, relying on his notes to refresh his memory due to his inability to recall specifics.

They presented the recording of his confession, wherein Ortiz declared, "The Monster came out of me."

Ortiz explained, "I wanted to clean up the streets ... since no one is going to do it."

Ortiz recounted, "We were driving to a place by Springfield, where I took Erika. Claudine lived in a hotel. In Springfield, where the projects are, turn to the left to get to the house that sells drugs."

Ranger Salinas remarked, "The first one was an accident. Ortiz started to clean the streets with Claudine" What tip about this case did Emilio give the Texas Ranger Salinas?

Ranger Salinas's responsibilities included assisting Webb County. He conducted 60 interviews, searched businesses, and followed numerous leads. When ADA Jacaman inquired if Salinas needed a search warrant for vehicular searches, Salinas asserted that he did not, as he had obtained consent to search cars, houses, and businesses.

At the crime scene of Melissa Ramirez, three casings were discovered. Trooper Hernandez informed Ranger Salinas of a kidnapped female. Erika Peña provided information about her assailant, his truck, and his residence, noting that she left her pink purse in his truck. Erika reported that she was assaulted by David, who was armed. The incident occurred at Stripes, located on San Bernardo Avenue.

Ranger Salinas observed that JD's truck was abandoned and contained two Tall Boys (beers), a pink purse, and an empty holster. Although he photographed the truck to document its condition and contents, he did not conduct a search at Stripes or remove any items from the vehicle. The photographs did not clearly show the empty holster, as it was too distant.

During Ortiz's interaction with his attorney, he questioned the photographs taken by Ranger Salinas. Salinas captured 15 photographs in 15 minutes and then transported the truck to Webb County. Ortiz, who was also observing the officer behind him, noted the use of the document, which was not intended as an inventory.

Although a pistol was found in the truck, Ranger Salinas maintained that the form was not for inventory purposes and reiterated that he did not search the truck or perform an inventory since he did not see the pistol. Ortiz was arrested around midnight and charged with evading arrest. Salinas instructed Ugarte to search Ortiz's truck.

Ranger Salinas's interrogation training was extensive, and he was familiar with Ortiz's occupation and mannerisms. Under oath, Salinas stated that he advised Ortiz of his Miranda rights. Although Salinas is not a medical doctor or a board-certified psychiatrist, he claimed that Ortiz did not exhibit signs of a mental breakdown. Ortiz refused to sign the Miranda waiver, instead writing "Refused to sign," but Salinas indicated that Ortiz nodded his head, signaling a waiver of his rights. Salinas emphasized that no promises were made during the interrogation.

Regarding blackouts, Ortiz mentioned he had PTSD, but Salinas declared that Ortiz did not experience blackouts.

I thoroughly reviewed the entire confession video and at no point did I observe Ortiz nodding his head up and down or explicitly waiving his rights during his confession. Nonetheless, Ortiz did choose to speak and disclose everything, effectively waiving his rights. The act of speaking constitutes a waiver of rights.

Ortiz appeared to be falling asleep during the interrogation. A pertinent question is whether Ortiz was on or off his medications at that time. Ranger Salinas advised Ortiz to "put in a good word—reveal the information to the DA."

Ortiz requested that his wife be prevented from traveling to Laredo from San Antonio and also asked for a photograph of his family. It was Ortiz's idea to surrender his phone and he mentioned his pension to Ranger Salinas. Both Calderon and Ranger Salinas signed the waiver of Ortiz's rights form.

Ortiz expressed that he did not want law enforcement to forcibly enter his home by kicking down the door; instead, he preferred that they use keys. During the interrogation, Ortiz also stated that he was a member of law enforcement. He requested that his wife be located or contacted to remain in San Antonio with their children.

Ortiz provided Ranger Salinas with the password to his phone so that family pictures could be accessed. Additionally, Ortiz handed over the keys to his house and consented to a DNA sample. Ranger Salinas testified that he believed Ortiz waived his rights due to his cooperative behavior. Notably, Ortiz never requested an attorney. ADA Jacaman interpreted Ortiz's actions—surrendering his cell phone, password, keys, and DNA—as equivalent to waiving his rights.

Ranger Salinas also mentioned that Ortiz purchased beer shortly after the murders. He admitted needing to refer to his notes to refresh his memory during court testimony. Despite maintaining a straight poker face, Salinas stated that Ortiz was not experiencing a mental breakdown, which justified the continuation of the interview. Salinas stated that Ortiz bought three Tall Boys (beer) at the gas station; Ortiz is seen on camera at the left entrance.

Subsequent to Erika's escape, Ranger Salinas stated, "There was nothing unusual about Juan David's behavior."

September 14, 2018

10:53 p.m.

Ortiz was observed wearing a khaki shirt, jeans, and a cap. He procured three beer cans.

10:54 p.m.

Ortiz exited the store, holding three beers as captured in the surveillance footage. He departed from the Murphy store.

10:56 p.m.

According to verbatim court testimony, Vasquez conducted a tire impression analysis at the Laredo Police Department, with Ranger Salinas present. The victims, comprising prostitutes, homeless individuals, and drug addicts, were all shot in the head with the same caliber firearm.

CONTINUING DECEMBER 5, 2022

5:45 p.m.

Ortiz glanced back and smiled at his mother.

DAY 2

2ND WEEK OF THE TRIAL

10:30 a.m.

DECEMBER 6, 2022

Mr. Daniel testified that in his professional opinion, all bullets were discharged from the same firearm. On February 12, 2019, the sealed envelope containing ballistic evidence was opened by the prosecution. Mr. Daniel conducted a thorough analysis of the evidence, examining nine cartridge cases identified as Federal 40 Smith & Wesson and 40 Smith Standard, commonly used by law enforcement.

These nine cartridge cases were recovered from the crime scene. His analysis determined that six projectiles were fired from the same handgun. Mr. Daniel claimed that this conclusion was based on his expert opinion.

The firearm in question was an Agent K, Heckler & Koch (H&K) P2000, chambered in .40 caliber. Mr. Daniel was unable to specify the type of steel used in the firearm.

During questioning by Perez, Mr. Daniel was asked how many cases he had analyzed, to which he replied, "Don't know?" He clarified that he conducted extensive research but lacked comparative data for his findings. Mr. Daniel did not conduct tests on the other H&K B-200 .40 caliber firearm.

Ortiz ogled me on two occasions and displayed a subtle grin during the proceedings. Mr. Daniel has testified as an expert witness for the State on twenty occasions.

The forensic analyst from Houston, responsible for preparing reports based on her own analysis, had her report admitted as evidence after Judge Hale overruled the defense's objection.

The impression found was covered in blood, which she cleaned up. A side-by-side analysis was conducted for Claudine Luera's case, categorized as follows: 2A - distinguished, 2B - most, 2C – blurry due to analysis being limited.

The doctor involved in the tire analysis concluded that any of the four tires or another similar tire could have been involved, as soil analysis is no longer conducted by their department. However, the practice continues elsewhere, though the doctor is unsure who currently performs such analyses.

Witness Dana Paola Sarquiz, employed in the Intelligence Division at Webb County Jail, monitors inmate phone calls with a team of seven analysts.

Dialogue: JD and the Author

Author: When I would talk to JD on the phone, I heard a guy laughing on the phone call. He might as well just talk on 3-way with us ... for real. I remember telling JD that I was giving him homework and I expected a book report in a week. The analysts burst out laughing. Talking to JD was a trip ... never had a dull moment with him. I always got that adrenaline-fun rush speaking to him, especially knowing that they were hearing and watching everything. You get to say things to make the officers listening laugh.

JD: You see ... they are listening to everything. They won't let me go out for my 1 hour of recreation.

JD was irritated.

CONTINUING DECEMBER 6, 2022

In 2018, Dana Sarquiz was not yet employed at Webb County Jail. She did not begin her employment until 2019.

On October 17, 2022, Ortiz departed for Bexar County. Prior to this, Ortiz had been incarcerated in Webb County Jail for four years. District Attorney Alaniz remarked to Dana Sarquiz, "Webb County Jail was practically Ortiz's home for four years. Consequently, you were privy to all his conversations and acquainted with everyone he communicated with." Sarquiz monitored all of Ortiz's phone calls. A CD disk labeled 238-239 contains a phone call made by Juan David Ortiz, during which Ortiz confessed to his wife over the phone.

November 6-7, 2018

During a phone conversation, Ortiz spoke to his wife about his statement:

Ortiz: "Les dije cómo pasó todo." (Translation: "I told them how everything happened.")

Ortiz continued, "They only have my statement. I'm worried about my statement. I want to make sure we are all on the same page, going to trial."

Daniella Ortiz replied, "You are my hope. Yes, we are all on the same page. With God, anything is possible."

"If that had been me and Juan David cheated on me with prostitutes, taking them to my home to use my bed to have sex, my shower, towel, and use the kitchen table to do drugs ... can you say 'Lorena Bobbit?' LOL! No pun intended."

CD 239 - July 18, 2020

During a thirty-minute phone conversation with his wife and children, Ortiz emphatically stated that he was not experiencing suicidal ideation. Throughout the call, Ortiz drew parallels between his situation and that of Casey Anthony. It is pertinent to note that Dana Sarquiz does not possess credentials as a voice recognition expert. Ortiz affectionately addressed his wife as "babe" and his children as "chipmunks." Notably, there were two such conversations prior to Ortiz's indictment.

District Attorney Alaniz plans to introduce new statements pertaining to Ortiz's mental state and emphasize his comparisons to Casey Anthony's case. The prosecution's strategy is to demonstrate that Ortiz was cognizant of his actions and not suffering from insanity.

To protect their privacy, the names of Ortiz's children have been altered. The pseudonyms used are Victoria and Siri for the two girls, and Daniel Joseph for the boy, totaling three children.

In this conversation, Ortiz discussed his statements, his children, and his hopes with his wife. Attorney Joey Tellez remarked that he could not take any action until Ortiz was indicted, citing the need for payment. During the call, Ortiz also mentioned the Casey Anthony case. At trial, he was visibly emotional and crying, covering his face with tissue to hide his vulnerability.

This particular phone call was played during an evidentiary hearing to determine its admissibility for the jury. The jurors did not witness Ortiz's emotional side; they only observed his stoic demeanor. This instance could have been pivotal for the defense to illustrate that Ortiz loves his children, cried for them, and possesses human emotions. Ortiz's mother was also visibly distressed, crying and holding up her Bible.

Author: I felt all her pain and energy.

Ortiz in the phone call: "The lawyer won't get money unless it's capital. There is no evidence, only a confession I made. Joey Tellez, my lawyer, said the DA would cave into public pressure, making it a capital murder case."

Narrative:

Today, they played the two conversations Ortiz had with his wife. I was mortified when Ortiz and his wife argued about me during the phone calls, referring to me as "that girl." Ortiz avoided using my name, so I was constantly referred to as "that girl." His wife was incensed because I had sent him a book about Casey Anthony. She seemed envious because Ortiz shared my opinions with her. Daniella Ortiz, Ortiz's wife, was adamant that Ortiz cease all communication with me. It didn't help that he boasted to her about my educational achievements.

I left the courtroom for a while, waiting for the phone calls to conclude. When I returned, I was both embarrassed and incensed with Ortiz. I made faces at him and spilled my water when he gawked at me.

DECEMBER 7, 2022

WEDNESDAY

2nd WEEK

DAY 3—FINAL DAY

The courtroom is packed with spectators awaiting Ortiz's sentencing. Ortiz had no defense, without any witnesses, medical experts to testify to his mental state or Veterans Affairs to validate his PTSD and prescribed medications. The defense failed to provide a psychological evaluation. During the trial, Ortiz's mother and Daniella Ortiz's phone numbers were inadvertently disclosed, causing significant distress. An officer reassured Ortiz's mother, exacerbating Ortiz's anxiety.

DECEMBER 7, 2022

12:10 p.m.

I pondered why Ortiz did not enter a plea of Not Guilty by Reason of Insanity or Temporary Insanity.

Ortiz had consistently claimed, "The VA, PTSD, and medications caused this!"

Judge Oscar Hale solemnly read the charges, evoking a palpable tension in the courtroom. The verdict resounded with gravity: "GUILTY on all charges."

A unanimous decision by the jury on Wednesday found Juan David Ortiz culpable of capital murder.

Hale's pronouncement echoed through the room: "We, the jury, find the defendant, Juan David Ortiz, guilty of the offense of capital murder, as charged in the indictment and as instructed in this charge."

Following the verdict, Judge Hale proceeded to deliver the sentence:

"As you are aware, and I trust your legal counsel has duly apprised you, the charge of capital murder carries an automatic penalty of life imprisonment without the possibility of parole."

When the guilty verdict was pronounced, DA Alaniz visibly moved his right arm up and down in affirmation, exclaiming, "Yes."

Doctors should have been called to testify on Ortiz's behalf, yet he had no defense. The prosecution presented testimony from 30 witnesses.

Karina Rios delivered the closing statements for the prosecution, emphasizing their pursuit:

"They desire justice for his intentional acts," she declared.

Ortiz is accused of committing at least two murders, and he appeared visibly serious throughout the proceedings. "Four times," Rios continued, "he stated, 'I was cleaning up the streets.'"

The question arises: Why did DA Alaniz refrain from presenting the closing argument?

Ortiz used the term "a monster" verbatim.

The defense failed to introduce a PowerPoint presentation, unlike the prosecution.

Issues of reasonable doubt and witness credibility were central to the proceedings.

Joel Perez, representing the defense, passionately argued:

"When the police violate Ortiz's rights, they violate our rights. Getting off on a technicality—it's either yes or no. Jurors, you have the right to know if his rights were violated. David's confession—was it involuntary? The State didn't obtain a search warrant; they violated the law. 'We are a nation of laws.' Jurors took an oath to follow the law. The law applies to all of us—good or bad, including police officers. Noe Hernandez was prevented from reading Ortiz's rights. They put Ortiz in a controlled environment. Were Juan David Ortiz's rights violated? Yes. Investigators take classes on how to testify. It all comes down to this—do you want your rights violated?

Inducement—look at the guy in front of you. They induced him improperly. He was under duress. The statement was involuntary. Rights are not privileges; they are yours! Seizure of property, bad police tactics—this is not a popularity contest. The vehicle was seized for 4th Amendment purposes. The minute they opened that truck, it was a search. Inventory or search—there is no such thing as preservation. An illegal search means the gun can't be used. There was no inventory search; they made up a preservation photo, which constituted a search. Ranger Salinas got ahead of himself, and now he is stuck. They manipulated the gun and removed the revolver.

Reasonable doubt, warrantless searches: If you have a doubt, the gun can't be used. Did Ortiz have the mental capacity at the time of the confession? Convict him of murder individually. Consider his history and who he was. Don't label him a serial killer. Give him individual murders."

DA Alaniz stated, "Erika is the probable cause (by aggravated assault). Interviews are cat and mouse."

DA Alaniz affirmed, "There was never any mental breakdown. I've disgraced the uniform. I've disgraced the country. I've disgraced the blue. Doing this for a long time. Double life! The monster came out of me. Ortiz's own words—"

DA Alaniz lauds Erika Peña as "the hero," asserting, "She was the key to break open the case."

DA Alaniz presented photographs of Melissa Ramirez and Claudine Luera.

DA Alaniz described the victims as having been "beaten with blunt force trauma."

DA Alaniz exclaimed, "Self-proclaimed monster! All because of his dirty needs."

DA Alaniz's oration is characterized by his theatricality; he exhibits pedagogical flair in narrating this case to the jury.

DA Alaniz displayed a photograph of Janelle Ortiz to the jury. DA Alaniz stated, "Didn't put up a fight—"

DA Alaniz screamed, "He was on the hunt."

DA Alaniz declared, "Mr. Daniel said science doesn't lie."

DA Alaniz replayed the video of Erika fleeing from Ortiz.

DA Alaniz proclaimed, "Juan David Ortiz disgraced the uniform, the country, the blue, and his family—for his own selfish needs."

DA Alaniz affirmed, "Erika has courage."

Chaos from 1:00 a.m. to 2:30 a.m.

Upon arrest, District Attorney Alaniz emphasized that law enforcement officers treated the individual with dignity and respect. Detectives Calderon and Salinas pursued truth and justice relentlessly. "The person was involved with Erika as a client and something more—a relationship."

Joel Perez pointed out consistencies and parallels in the case, highlighting significant reasonable doubt. He argued for prioritizing the preservation of rights, asserting, "Preserving our constitutional rights outweighs letting one individual evade justice due to a technicality."

DA Alaniz detailed the discovery of an H&K firearm and 37 rounds in the vehicle, noting, "All they have is my statement ... in a jail call to his wife."

DA Alaniz informed, "In the jury form, the verdict appears on the final page. Put Ortiz guilty of capital murder."

Two jurors were dismissed, awaiting jury deliberation.

Joel Perez stated, "Find Ortiz guilty of murder for each count."

District Attorney Alaniz and Joel Perez conversed and smiled while waiting for the jury to deliver its verdict.

It is 5:26 p.m. The District Attorney continues to glance at me. I invoke the Fifth Amendment ... no pun intended.

At 5:56 p.m., the jury reached a verdict.

The courtroom brims with tension—

6:00 p.m.—No verdict

7:36 p.m.—Verdict

—Guilty of Capital Murder—

All jurors proclaimed, "GUILTY".

Ortiz did not issue a statement. Following this, family statements were delivered. Ortiz received an automatic sentence of life without parole. When Judge Hale inquired whether Ortiz intended to appeal his case, he affirmed. Immediately upon the judge's announcement of the verdict, Juan David Ortiz was handcuffed by the bailiff, in a manner reminiscent of Hollywood drama, for the cameras. Ortiz's mother wept audibly as the bailiff placed the handcuffs on him, her sobs echoing in the courtroom. Her anguish was palpable, and as I gestured to Ortiz to call me, using my right hand, he glanced my way. I desired to hear his perspective on the unfolding events.

Ortiz met my gaze, rolling his eyes, seeming impatient with the numerous statements being directed at him. Meanwhile, his mother continued weeping, comforted by his twin sisters as the victims' families delivered their impact statements. More than 16 families expressed their condemnation in these statements.

STATEMENTS BY THE FAMILIES

Christina Benavides, mother of Melissa Ramirez

"Maldito asesino. Eres un monstruo. Tus hijos siempre serán los hijos de un asesino."

Translation in English: "Damn murderer. You are a monster. Your children will always be the children of a murderer."

—Christina Benavides

The comments made by Christina Benavides, particularly targeting Ortiz's children, were exceptionally harsh. Children are innocent and should not bear the burden of their parents' actions. Despite Ortiz's self-proclaimed identity as a "monster," he evidently loves his children, which demonstrates that he possesses some emotional capacity, unlike individuals who abandon or harm their offspring. He is not the type to hurt children; his actions categorize him as a missionary killer.

Joey Cantu, brother of Guiselda Hernandez

Joey Cantu's speech resonated deeply with the public. Here is his poignant address:

"She's all I had. You took the last family member of my family. She was going to talk you out of suicide. It would be so easy to hate you—too easy; *I don't hate you; I don't hate you at all, but I hate what you did.* Here is the irony: Roughly 26 1/2 years ago, I stood where you now stand—accused and convicted of murder—sentenced to 40 years in the Texas Department of Criminal Justice. It has been 22 years and 11 months of my life in prison—from the age of 15—to the age of 38. When I was granted parole, the sister of the victim wrote to me and told me ... that she forgave me for what I had done—and that I should forgive myself as well. And—I find myself in front of the person who— killed my little sister.

And I want you to know that I forgive you, and I hold no ill will towards you ... man. I pray that one day you find the peace that you have gripped away from all of us. You spoke of God's ability for miracles. Well, your miracle is that you get to continue living—to continue to see and hear from your loved ones, while we no longer can—when in any other circumstance, you would be facing the death sentence. And know that it was me—the brother of Guisela—who asked the DA to consider going without the death penalty ... because your family has suffered as well.

No parent should watch their child die—even yours. I leave you with the words of my sister: 'No matter what you've done, it doesn't matter. God will forgive you, and God loves you. May you find peace and freedom in Him'. But ... I will forever wonder if—maybe ... Erika was not who she was—if Erika was not a prostitute and a drug addict ... if swifter action could have been taken? Would they have believed her if she was an outstanding citizen? Would it have taken 4 hours to find him—3 hours—2 hours—however long it took? It's not entirely your fault; we were failed at times by the justice system too."

—Joey Cantu

I understand Joey Cantu's perspective; however, Erika Peña did receive respect from law enforcement. They utilized her as a star witness, and District Attorney Alaniz referred to her as a hero. Laredo is not equipped for an emergency management crisis. If a mass shooting were to occur, the city lacks the hospital capacity and necessary preparedness. Law enforcement had to regroup and obtain a search warrant. Moreover, the attorneys argued that law enforcement lacked a search warrant for Ortiz's vehicle, thus violating his rights.

Considering the Uvalde school shooting, the protracted response time led to the deaths of many children due to inadequate planning and preparation. Nevertheless, Joey Cantu's viewpoint is valid. Had Erika Peña been part of an elite, affluent family, such as the Cuellars—the "Kennedys of Laredo"—law enforcement might have employed helicopters to locate Ortiz.

Video evidence indicates that the Department of Public Safety (DPS) believed Erika and did not ignore her. She was taken seriously, received justice, and her voice was heard. Law enforcement, alongside Erika Peña, endeavored to locate Ortiz, but he had already fled. It became a protracted pursuit.

Ortiz's mother was visibly distressed, crying as she said, "Mijo ... I love you," before he left. The metaphorical impact of each victim impact statement on her heart was palpable. Each time a family member expressed their hatred and wished death upon Ortiz, his mother wept. I observed Ortiz's mother, uncle, and twin sisters exiting through a side door; they were eager to leave, and I empathized with them. Ortiz's mother appeared to have sprained her ankle in the parking lot. I saw her on the ground, surrounded by her family, and chose to continue to my vehicle to avoid adding to their stress. My timing, as always, was ...

WHATABURGER

I find it highly amusing that, following his confession, JD was casually eating a burger and fries, drinking from a straw, while law enforcement filmed the scene. The subsequent video sparked a flurry of online comments, many of which were equally humorous.

Here are a few of the remarks:

- "The brazen audacity to have his left pinky raised while putting on condiments."

- "Whataburger... so good, it'll make you confess to murder."

- "Oh my god, he eats food like a human—what a monster."

- "He was licking his chops."

- "He murdered that meal."

- "The guy in the back looking at him like—you took my meal."

The public fixated on JD's meal, an act that he could never have anticipated would become national news. This phenomenon illustrates a common tactic used by law enforcement: making a suspect wait for eight to eleven hours before offering a meal, thereby encouraging a confession.

JANUARY 24, 2024

Author: I saw the video of you eating a burger. That was your last good meal.

JD: Yes, they left the part of me eating a burger, but they took out the part where I asked for an attorney twice and they were bargaining with me—quid pro quo.

Author: Did you know you were being recorded?

JD: No—I didn't know I was being recorded. The meal from Whataburger was part of the bargaining that they did with me. I didn't have a full meal until 10-11 hours after the interrogation was over. I was handcuffed to a chair and couldn't leave or terminate the interrogation—even though I asked for an attorney three times.

A couple from New Braunfels walked into the courtroom, visibly vexed, and remarked, "He has no defense; I could have done a better job at defending him." Another individual commented, "JD has mental issues that could have been used in the trial." Someone else suggested, "He could have multiple personality disorder."

During JD's trial, I observed several national media representatives conversing during a break in the hallway. I overheard them saying, "Man, he's not talking to anyone in the media." I interjected, "Ha-ha, I have communicated with him," and smiled. However, I was not media, strictly speaking. Throughout the trial, JD's mother consistently held a book in her hands.

According to Erika Peña's statements at trial and national news reports, Juan David Ortiz's infatuation with Erika Peña resembled the plot of "Pretty Woman," albeit in a Laredo-style context.

JANUARY 24, 2024

Author: Were you in love, obsessed, in a relationship, or had feelings for Erika Peña?

JD: I was not in love, obsessed, in a relationship, or had any feelings for Erika Peña.

Author: What is your type?

JD: I like women who are petite, tanned skin ... and are highly educated, intelligent, and wear glasses. Intelligence is what turns me on the most in a woman.

CHAPTER 6
CONVERSATIONS WITH JUAN DAVID ORTIZ

JD: I was very patriotic and loved my country.

Author: I love *The Big Bang Theory*.

JD: You know that's my favorite show.

Author: Which one? *The Big Bang Theory*? Really? That's my favorite show.

JD: I told you before that I like that show.

JD: I think she's so attractive.

Author: Who? The politician who wears glasses? So ... then you like nerdy chicks with glasses?

Author: So—you have a type? I thought you had another type. That's what the national media says ...

JD: That's not true. Don't believe everything they say.

Author: I have a huge crush on Mike Johnson, the Speaker of the House. It's his cute face and those glasses. LOL.

JD: I am nothing like Mike Johnson.

JD: How did you know that I like Saint Paul?

Author: I didn't know ... I just felt that you would like it. Something told me to send it to you.

JD: My life is over.

Author: Did you ever do (carne asada) barbecue on Sundays?

JD: Yes ... but I would burn the meat when I would do BBQ.

JD possesses a comprehensive knowledge of the Bible, demonstrating familiarity with its verses and teachings.

JD: I'm working out and the V-Cut is already showing on my lower abs.

Author: Really ...

JD: Yes, I'm getting the big V cut. I wake up at 4:00 a.m. to 5:00 a.m., and then I fall asleep by 7:00 p.m. to 7:30 p.m.; I wake up super early, then I go to sleep early. My day is very repetitive; I do the same thing every day. There's nothing new going on with me or my life; my life is very routine. If I don't talk to you every day and I call you in a week, just remember that there is nothing new going on with me.

JD: I received fan mail from people telling me: "We're with you; we understand; keep fighting; keep up the fight."

JD: That makes me happy ... that I have fans. I got letters from "big media investigator" companies. I mean ... big timers. I got a letter from a freelance author, but I am not responding to anyone—just you.

Author: Well, I'm not media. You better not be talking to other media—because I will get jealous ... LOL.

JD: Don't worry ... I'm not.

Author: Did you ever get any female ... nude pics?

Author: You got some sexy pics ... huh? Were they all provocative?

JD: Yes ... I also got a picture from a woman holding a red rose, another 41-year-old that was stubborn and wrote me 5 times. I had to tell her that I was appealing my case and could only speak to my family to make her stop. They all tell me the same thing—that they want to write to me, get to know me, and be my pen pals—and want to hear my side of the story. Some of the women were from Arizona, Tennessee, and Indiana. None of those women got my attention; I'm not interested in them or in getting to know them.

Author: You have fans now? I thought they didn't allow nude pics in TDCJ (Texas Department of Criminal Justice) LOL! Shout out to these women ... you got rejected! Ha-ha!

JD: I'm watching this show now ... that I like on my tablet; it's called—*The Chosen*—

Author: I like that show too; that's one of my favorite shows.

JD: I'm here with other big-time high-profile cases ... like big time; you should contact them ... like I mean big-time high-profile cases ... like mine.

Author: I don't know who they are; I've never heard of them.

Author: What? You're pimping me out to go write their books or what?

Author: You know how the Webb County sheriff's officers are all short and you're tall? I bet you could take them all out with your training skills from war, navy, and marines ... if you wanted to. I'm not saying you are—I'm saying if you wanted to.

JD: Yeah ...

JD: I never talked to you about my case; you were never part of my case.

Author: Yeah ... I know we never talked about your case, and I was not ... part of your case.

JD: My wife is still with me after everything.

JD: My wife sent me some white tennis shoes to the jail here.

JD: My family is everything; that's what I've learned. And they're the only ones that are there for me during all this; my family is everything, and they are first.

Author: I don't know how to shoot a gun.

JD: I would have shown you how.

JD's wife remains with him, allowing her to access his benefits and avoid testifying in his appeal.

Spousal immunity, codified in Rule 504(b) of the Texas Rules of Evidence, is a long-standing doctrine that prevents an individual from being compelled to testify against their spouse in criminal proceedings. This rule was established to uphold the integrity and sanctity of marriage. In Texas, two specific provisions safeguard couples from potentially incriminating one another: the Confidential Communication Privilege and the Privilege Not to Testify in a Criminal Case. Collectively, these provisions are known as "Spousal Privileges" or "Husband-Wife Privileges," as delineated in Rule 504 of the Texas Rules of Evidence.

JD contacted me in tears, expressing his longing for his children, particularly because Sundays were traditionally family days. He requested that I write a book about him for his children.

JD: God is going to help me get out to be free; I'm going to get my freedom. God is going to GET ME OUT OF HERE.

JD: I was praying inside to God in court—during my trial.

JD: I got fan mail from lots of media—people saying that they are with me.

JD: Two ladies went to the Webb County Jail; one was saying that I needed a mother figure and the other said she was my attorney.

While JD was at Webb County Jail under suicide watch, he took it upon himself to retrieve paperwork outside his cell and complete the checklist independently, as officers occasionally neglected their duties, according to former high-ranking officers who were present at the time. JD himself confirmed this when questioned.

JD is characterized as intelligent, exceedingly respectful, and maintains a professional and formal demeanor; he consistently addressed me by my title. His profound respect stems from his high regard for education, which he perceives as significant, and he extended this respect to me due to my academic degrees and educational background.

Officers at Webb County Jail displayed antagonistic behavior towards JD, withholding his books and mail. They even prohibited him from retaining his Bible when he was transferred to TDCJ after sentencing. JD was misled by Webb County Jail personnel who falsely claimed that the books I sent him via Amazon were property of the jail and demanded their return. This misinformation was conveyed to JD by "the chaplain," despite the fact that I was the sender of those books. Only after a complaint was lodged with the Texas Commission on Jail Standards did Webb County Jail administration relent and allow JD access to his mail and books. Their actions appeared punitive, aimed at further isolating JD despite his vulnerable state on suicide watch.

JD: When I was in Iraq, I was at the front of the line. All of a sudden, boom ... boom ... boom. We were the ones who would throw the bombs.

JD exhibits a demeanor characterized by calmness, yet he can swiftly transition to a state of intense anxiety.

Author: Did you have an iPhone or Android?

JD: I had an iPhone ... the big phones.

Author: How are your kids?

JD: My kids are small; they don't know what is going on.

JD: The media followed my little twin sisters around their college.

Author: Damn ... stalkers. That's harassment.

Author: Did you read a lot of books when you were outside?

JD: I didn't read books when I was in the outside world; I didn't have the time. It wasn't until I got locked up that I started to read books and watch television.

JD: Elijah went to heaven—alive. The hill to the east of the Jordan River—opposite Jericho— is believed to be the site from which Elijah was taken up to heaven on a chariot of fire.

Author: Wow ... I didn't know. I'm going to the Jordan River. I went to Jericho. Thank you for telling me this.

JD: You have little woman syndrome ...because you are feisty.

Author: What ... LOL!

JD: You are my angel ... my Victoria's Secret Angel ... LOL!

Author: LOL!

JD: One of the officers here told me to be careful with you because you are a reportera Cubana (Cuban reporter). He saw your picture when—I put it on my wall with gum. I took it down when the officer told me that about you; I didn't like him seeing you ... I don't want others to see you.

Author: No, I'm not. He is confusing me with this other chick that comes out in the news.

JD: Before I left the facility, I threw everything away in the trash ... so nobody could have your letters or pics. Almost all the books ... I passed on here for others to use and read.

JD: I have my books outside my cell. I'm only allowed to have a few at a time. A night shift officer passed by my cell and said I had a good book—and he took it with him. Burgos wanted your book. He saw it outside my cell—and is bored with the books here ... since they are all religious.

Author: I think it's hilarious that you all are fighting for books ... ha-ha!

Author: What's that screaming noise in the background?

JD: It's Burgos ... he is bored.

Author: No pos—wow ... damn ... he is loud.

JD: Somebody sent me a large amount of money and put it in my account. I'm not complaining.

Author: Oh ... I wonder who it is?

JD: I'm trying to figure it out.

Author: What happened to your house here in Laredo?

JD: That house is gone; they got rid of everything. And they donated my books to Goodwill. All my books ... library ... are gone. That's what hurt me the most ... my books.

Author: When did you get your bird tattoos on your chest?

JD: I got my bird tattoos when I was in the Navy.

JD: When I stayed in the Webb County Jail, I saw the name Miguel Angel Venegas in my cell. The jailers told me that an inmate had hung himself here, committing suicide.

The staff's actions, sharing unnecessary details with JD while he was on suicide watch, seemed intended to provoke fear or induce panic attacks, which was unnecessary given his vulnerable state.

JD: In my cell, the lights flicker on and off by themselves. I haven't been able to sleep. I put the blanket over my face to avoid the light in my cell.

JD: I had to cast out the demons—in Jesus's name. If I told you all the stories that happened to me before about casting out demons—the things I saw ...

JD: I'm afraid to take my sleeping pills; I can't talk about it.

JD: When I was younger, I saw a pastor at a church cast out demons in a church; I saw things.

JD: They haven't taken me to take a shower. I feel so disgusting. I've been in the same gown for days. It's harder for me to exercise in this gown without underwear ... like doing pushups and sit-ups.

Author: So ... you're bouncing around ... literally. Freestyling ... hey, at least it's good for your sperm count. You are flashing the camera ... Ha-ha. If it was me, I would be giving them a show on purpose ... to make them laugh LOL.

JD: LOL ... You're hilarious ...

JD: Perez told me that you were billing him for the phone calls I made to you on a line-item—itemized bill.

Author: He is lying. That's not true; I never charged your attorney ... that's a huge lie. I'm so sure. I don't even know how to do that. Now I want to learn how to do a line-item—itemized bill. Let me google it. It's true what they say ... lawyers are really LIARS.

Author: You like bikes and bike riding?

JD: Yes, that's how I got huge legs. My legs were ... huge. I would have shown you how to ride a bike and we could have gone bike riding together—I love bikes.

JD expressed in a letter to me, "Your persistence is what got my attention." He holds a deep appreciation for education and holds those with degrees in high regard.

JD: Don't say bad words ... hey, don't talk like that; You can't talk like that ... you have an education. You can't sound all ghetto.

JD would become triggered if I did not communicate appropriately (slang or bad words), possibly due to past experiences that have left him with PTSD related to interactions with women.

JD: It's in the Bible about false prophets—talking about horoscopes or your birth signs; don't talk about your horoscope.

Author: 22 is my favorite number—the day of your birthday.

JD, a Gemini like several infamous serial killers such as Dahmer (no pun intended), would often provide me with advice on potential job opportunities in Laredo.

JD: My family is very positive and nice to me.

JD would often enter panic mode with me, fearing that I might have gone to the media or that our phone calls were being recorded for his appeal. This transition from calm and collected to anxious and panicked would occur suddenly, causing him distress. He tended to overthink things deeply at times, which exacerbated his anxiety. After such incidents, I would sometimes become upset with him and accuse him of unjust suspicions, but I regretted reacting that way and would apologize to him afterward. I realized I had no right to judge him, as I wasn't in his position and couldn't fully understand his circumstances.

I empathized with JD's situation of being incarcerated and feeling distrustful of others, including the media. I sympathized with his mindset and the challenges he faced in isolation, where he struggled with trusting anyone. It seemed like JD had two distinct personas: one where he was his usual self, and another where he was overwhelmed by panic and symptoms reminiscent of PTSD.

Despite these challenges, JD consistently treated me with respect. It deeply troubled me when he confided that nobody had ever made him feel as bad or hurt his feelings as I had. This realization left me feeling remorseful and guilty, as if I had inadvertently caused distress to a man dealing with isolation and PTSD.

JD: Once this is all over—trial, I will tell you everything that happened ... what happened. Nothing is like it seems. Quiero hablar contigo bien, no asi.

Translation: I want to talk to you right, not like this—with no recordings—without them listening to everything.

Author: I am going to give you homework, and I expect you to do a book report in a week. What was that? Can you hear the guy laughing in our call? Is he on three-way with us? I am trying to make you laugh, so you can feel better with the professor's book report—joke.

JD: Yeah, they are listening.

JD exhibits a forgiving nature, devoid of grudges. In contrast, I have friends who harbor lifelong grudges against me due to differing views on Biden and politics, despite my neutral stance and lack of idolization towards Biden akin to JFK.

JD generally maintains a calm demeanor. However, his PTSD-induced panic sporadically surfaces, triggered by overthinking minor details, leading to bouts of worry and anxiety.

JD: If I cut you off cold turkey, don't get mad at me; I don't want you to hate me—because everyone already hates him. I might not be able to talk to you anymore because I'm appealing my case ... and they are using everything I say against me. You are not a part of my case—and have nothing to do with my case ... but ... I still have to listen to my attorneys. I have to do what my lawyers say.

JD: My family is my priority—they are the most important thing to me.

JD: You didn't write to me on a letterhead. I want you to use a letterhead when you write to me the next time; I am used to letterheads.

Author: Are you serious? You are kidding ... right? You want me to be super professional and not be lax. You are so picky. Fine ... I took the time to find a letterhead for you ... with a bird on it—no pun intended.

JD cannot be universally categorized as malevolent. Throughout the majority of his life, JD exhibited commendable behavior. He maintained a composed demeanor, save for the occasions when he engaged in acts of homicide and embarked upon a spree of killings.

JD: From the day I was born, right up until February, I was a squared away bastard.

JD: They took me to get a haircut here at Webb County Jail. An inmate cuts our hair. I had many officers escorting me—there was a guy who had to go to the side of the wall ... when I passed by; inmates who were walking by—had to stand against the wall ... when I passed by. I thought the officers were protecting me against them—the inmates against the wall. But then I realized ... the officers were protecting them—the inmates against the wall— against me. And that's when it hit me ... the situation that I was in—that I was the "dangerous" one.

JD: I have to buy Ramen soups—because the food here doesn't fill me up.

JD: I'm on my knees talking to you right now—because that's the only way I can reach the phone; I have to be on my knees to talk.

JD: In TDCJ ... I have to get strip searched to talk to you ... on the other phone. I'm calling you from my cell—from my tablet ... because I don't feel like getting strip searched right now—to go use the other phone. This is the first time my tablet works in here—when I called you; that's a first—it's a miracle. It has never worked in here before.

JD: The officers at Webb County Jail bring drugs to the inmates. There was a riot the other time—

JD: I had big legs when I was outside ... since I used to go bike riding—my legs were huge.

JD: God is going to get me out of here. And He is giving me my freedom; I will get my freedom ... one day. I have hope. That's why I tell you that I'm not worried about lawyers ... I have faith in God. I know I'm getting my freedom ... someday.

JD: You did a fantastic job with your bikini picture in your book.

Author: Thanks ... I appreciate it.

JD: I saw you in a fight on television ... once. You were sitting at a table.

Author: You saw me? LOL ... I was sitting in the front with my friend and some politicians.

JD: I recognized you.

Author: I was a little—happy ... LOL ...

Author: Can you draw?

JD: No, I can't draw.

Author: Me neither.

Author: Do you like comic books? *Star Trek* and *Star Wars*?

JD: No ... Burgos is the one who gets those and likes all that. They send those to him ... all his "amigas" (female friends).

JD: I miss my kids. Today is Sunday; it's supposed to be family day. I want you to do a book for my kids.

In my memory, there was a moment when JD called me in tears, pleading for a book to be created for his children. Frankly, I empathized with him deeply, hearing his raw emotional state over the phone, his concern palpable for his children.

Author: I wish I hadn't met that Jewish guy; he was a huge mistake.

JD: It was supposed to happen; it was already written in the book. God wanted it to happen ... He let it happen.

Author: Really ... so it's not my fault? I keep blaming myself, thinking how I messed up—should have seen it coming and avoided it. So, I couldn't have changed things, and it was going to happen anyway?

JD: No, it's not your fault. It was going to happen anyway; It was destined to happen—God let it happen.

Author: Thank you for giving me closure ... I feel so much better now—your words made a huge difference in my life. I was carrying all that inside me. You said it so easy and made it so simple. I was searching for the answer—why—and the answer came when I least expected it.

Author: My two male cousins said they hung out with you—that you all went fishing and to my cousin's house. They said you were a good guy, behaved well, trustworthy, and very quiet.

JD: I didn't hang out with them that much.

Author: ... okay ...

JD reported a series of concerning issues at Webb County Jail. The conditions within the facility are rapidly deteriorating, exacerbated by frequent breakdowns of the air conditioning on the third floor. Inmates are confined in cells devoid of windows, and conditions on the first floor are uncomfortably cold. A water boil notice created further complications, prompting Sheriff Martin Cuellar to distribute water bottles to inmates following public outcry on a website and Facebook. This response came amidst Laredo's sweltering temperatures exceeding 100 degrees. Sheriff Cuellar's policy also prohibits fans in inmate cells, despite concerns raised by the Texas Commission on Jail Standards regarding contaminated water consumption among inmates.

Tragically, two inmates lost their lives due to overdose incidents. Ashley Nicole Castro, aged 30, passed away on October 9, 2021, from an overdose of withdrawal medication (methadone). Christopher Torres-Garcia, aged 34, similarly overdosed on December 13, 2021.

In a distressing incident, Brian James McQuarrie, an inmate at Webb County Jail, attempted suicide. While Laredo Medical Center assessed him as stable, Brian James McQuarrie, aged 67, tragically succumbed to self-inflicted injuries on April 28, 2022.

Furthermore, allegations surfaced that six employees falsified records, including Sgt. Mendoza, Nurse Ruiz (female), and Officer Contreras. Investigations by the FBI or Texas Rangers are ongoing.

Officer Hector Rodriguez faced accusations of engaging in sexual relations with two female inmates at Webb County Jail. Investigations revealed incidents occurring at cells 101 or 102 within an area known as Vestibule 101 or 102. Surveillance cameras were non-functional during these incidents, which came to light following an outcry from one inmate who requested medical attention.

Additionally, inmates at the facility face severe hardships, lacking basic provisions within their cells. The entire facility also endured a COVID-19 outbreak, further compounding the challenges faced by inmates and staff alike.

This detailed account underscores the urgent need for comprehensive reforms at Webb County Jail to ensure the safety, well-being, and dignity of its inmates, as well as to restore public trust in the institution.

JD: "Are you writing all this down?"

Author: "Yes..."

In discussing the conditions and events within the prison system, several critical points arise:

Inmates, per regulations, are allocated three hours weekly for recreation, yet often fail to access this entitlement. Reports suggest that access to recreation remains a challenge for many incarcerated individuals.

Water quality concerns within the prison environment have surfaced, with inmates reportedly consuming substandard water, raising health and safety questions.

During Hector Rodriguez's official duty, he allegedly engaged in sexual relations with two female inmates, a violation of ethical and legal standards.

Tragically, Ashley Nicole's death occurred under circumstances where the inmate's requests for medical assistance were allegedly denied, prompting questions about the adequacy of healthcare provision within correctional facilities.

Furthermore, these deaths transpired within a mere three to four months of each other, prompting scrutiny into systemic issues and operational protocols.

The political campaign of Ponce Trevino for Sheriff emerges against this backdrop, raising questions about accountability and reform within the law enforcement system.

JD: "Did you get everything?"

Author: "Yes—"

JD: "Let's go over it again—"

Hector Rodriguez, an officer involved in a scandal, allegedly engaged in inappropriate conduct with female inmates. A young female inmate tragically overdosed on a methadone pill and subsequently died. These incidents occurred three to four months apart, highlighting ongoing issues with drug management and inmate safety.

McQuarrie suffered a severe head injury after banging his head on concrete, necessitating treatment at Laredo Medical Center. In response to this incident, six employees faced termination for falsifying records, exposing systemic failures in oversight and accountability.

In 2022, disturbing reports emerged from Mental Health cell block 3E, where inmates engaged in unsanitary behaviors, described colloquially as a "shit party." Three officers reportedly refused to address the situation, resulting in disciplinary actions. Janice Villarreal, one of the officers terminated for refusing to clean, subsequently filed a lawsuit for wrongful termination, citing inadequate equipment and hazardous conditions. Cesar Holguin and Pete Montemayor similarly refused to clean the cell block, aligning with Janice Villarreal's claims of inadequate resources. These incidents underscore systemic failures in sanitation protocols and workplace safety.

Regarding inmate welfare, there were reports of inadequate access to showers in the booking area, failing to meet the established hygiene standards of showering once every other day. The designated recreation time, three hours per week at El Patio, often falls short of what inmates are entitled to receive, impacting their mental and physical well-being. Juan David expressed frustration over the absence of an *inmate handbook* for three years, highlighting administrative deficiencies and potential legal oversights. Reports surfaced of inmates consuming contaminated water, raising significant health concerns within the facility. Mail delivery delays persisted, with some inmates experiencing up to two to three months delay in receiving their mail, impeding communication and legal correspondence. Allegations of price gouging at the commissary, where items such as Ramen Noodle Soup were priced significantly higher than market rates ($1.50 vs. $0.35), drew scrutiny. Notably, the commissary is operated by a Webb County employee, suggesting potential conflicts of interest and ethical concerns.

Shane "SeaWorld" Sowell, formerly employed with the Texas Commission on Jail Standards, left his position after attempting to implement reforms at Webb County Jail. Known for his adherence to protocols, Sowell's departure raises questions about institutional resistance to reform efforts and the maintenance of ethical standards within correctional facilities.

Author: I saw this hilarious video ... it tells you that when you get arrested, you need to *shut the fuck up* ... LOL!

JD: ... oh ...

Author: —you talked too much. You said enough—already ... I saw this video—and it's hilarious ...

Author: I'm not afraid of you.

JD: That's good that you're not afraid of me; you shouldn't be.

There were allegations that JD had orchestrated the murders of former Constable Rudy Rodriguez's prostitutes. This was purportedly due to Rudy's federal imprisonment resulting from attempting to coerce a prostitute across the U.S.-Mexico border. Furthermore, it was rumored that Rudy intended to return to Mexico to replenish those JD had allegedly murdered, given his role as a pimp, establishing a brothel in Laredo.

Author: Was Rudy Rodriguez, former constable, part of your case or involved with you? Was he the pimp? Did you pay or deal with him?

JD: No ... not at all. He has no involvement with me, and he has nothing to do with my case.

Juan David clarified the situation for me, which I found amusing. I struggle to imagine Rudy and JD together—JD as the dominant figure and Rudy as the influential player. Rudy, once possessing everything, suffered a downfall, losing his status, identity, and standing due to financial motives, avarice, and sexual indulgence. Rudy exhibits astute street smarts and embodies the archetype of an entrenched politician. Male judgment often falters when confronted with sexual allure, as exemplified by the cases of Juan David and Rudy.

JD: When Ponce Trevino was running for Sheriff, I made a sign with a piece of paper that said, "Ponce Trevino for Sheriff," and put it on my window ... right in front of the camera. They saw it ... LOL.

JD: When Ponce Trevino used to work here as the Sheriff's right hand, he was very fair with me; Trevino would always ask me if I got my mail and books, and if I needed anything ... he followed policies and was straight. I prefer Trevino to be Sheriff over the one we have right now.

JD: When there was a complaint with the Texas Commission on Jail Standards, the chaplain started singing and dancing hymns—religious songs in the halls here.

JD: The chaplain wanted the books back and told me they belonged to him. He said he got them for me to borrow.

Author: That's ridiculous ... the chaplain is stealing your books ... the ones I paid for and sent via Amazon for you. The audacity of this man—after he claims to be preaching about God. He is lying to you. I—bought those books. I know they are virtuous religious books ... but he doesn't have to take them from you. He gets paid good money—he can afford his own books.

JD: They didn't even let me take the blue Navy Bible you sent me. My family sent me a new and better Bible with explanations and lessons—Study Bible. It has more information to teach me the Bible.

In the context of JD's case, the deprivation of his religious liberties stands as a poignant violation. Denying a man access to his Bible while incarcerated raises profound ethical questions. Reflecting on a conversation with a trainer at TDCJ, based in Beeville, his assertion resonates: "Incarceration itself constitutes punishment; additional mistreatment is unwarranted." His admonition underscores the principle that correctional facilities should uphold humane treatment without undue abuse.

Seeking further understanding, I queried a criminal defense attorney about their defense of individuals accused of heinous crimes. Their response was unequivocal: "Regardless of their actions, inmates possess inherent rights that must be upheld within the confines of the justice system." This perspective challenged my previous notions, prompting a paradigm shift towards greater empathy and broader perspectives. Formerly holding a stringent view that inmates forfeited their entitlement to basic rights and legal representation, this interaction facilitated a transformation from narrow-mindedness to enlightened awareness.

Attorney: Yes, they're inmates ... but they are still somebody's family ... somebody's son ... somebody's brother ... somebody's father ... somebody's friend. They're still human; they just did bad things.

JD: I read my books starting from the last page first. I was not—expecting that swimming suit picture in your book. I was like ... wow!

Author: Thank you!

JANUARY 13, 2024

Conversations with Juan David Ortiz

JD: On 6/1/2022, Judge Hale had a *Change of Venue* hearing. Judge Hale held a very long hearing (about 2 hours) in order for the prosecution to file a controverting affidavit. We won based on default. The prosecution didn't produce these documents. ADA Maricela Jacaman testified as a witness for the prosecution that my case was old, didn't receive media attention, and wasn't getting media exposure. ADA Joaquin Rodriguez filed the controverting affidavit after the hearing started at 3:07 p.m.—not before this hearing.

The hearing was over and we won by default. Judge Hale refused to make a decision. It wasn't until my final pretrial hearing—on 8/17/202—that Judge Hale stated I got a *Change of Venue*. Between the time frame of 6/1/2022 to 8/17/2022, I was offered a plea bargain to accept life without parole and not have a trial—but I refused. My death penalty trial in San Antonio, Texas was going to cost 1.2 million to 1.5 million more dollars to Webb County. The DA went to ask the Commissioner's Court for half a million dollars to try my case in San Antonio—without the death penalty and life in prison without parole. Instead of taking 6 weeks for the jury selection process, the jury was selected in 3 hours. Joaquin Rodriguez was no longer working with the DA's office. He either got fired or quit—probably for making the costly mistake of not filing a *controverting affidavit* on time.

On the night of my arrest, I requested an attorney to Investigator Federico Calderon and Ranger Salinas. They both told me, "You aren't getting one." I refused to sign the Miranda rights. At the substation, I was told I would get first-degree murder—first four-degree murder. It's life with parole after 30 years. I was not in the *right state of mind*. They induced me. Joel Perez, Raymond Fuchs, Joey Tellez (my attorneys), Johnny Rodriguez (defense investigator), and Elizabeth Harvey (mitigation specialist) all knew that I didn't get an attorney ... even though I requested an attorney on the night of my arrest—3 times. I told them all for 4 years; I never stopped telling them. Harvey has emails showing that the Webb County Sheriff's Office denied her visits to see me at Webb County Jail.

On that night, I was legally parked; my truck was locked. The doors to my truck were locked. I had the keys in my pocket. Ranger Salinas didn't see my weapon in my truck. The firearm was in the glove compartment locked—not loaded. They opened the glove box compartment, loaded it, and put it on the door panel. They tampered with evidence ... staging the scene. I told everyone on my defense team this information. They went into my house without a warrant. Then they went in again with a warrant. Two times—I asked for an attorney when I went in. They affirmed "No." I declined to sign the Miranda rights and requested legal representation. Subsequently, I was restrained to a chair and unable to conclude the interrogation. The firearm was confirmed as unloaded. ADA Joaquin Rodriguez failed to file the controverting affidavit promptly, resulting in a *Change of Venue* granted by default. Jury selection, which was projected to take six weeks, was completed in only three hours.

ADA Josh Davila knows what the prosecution team was doing. They deleted the part where I requested an attorney in the video. Davila talked to me in the holding cell—next to the court. I told him that I requested an attorney and never got one. Davila is a good guy. He left because he wanted to save his law license; he knew what they were doing to me was wrong. They did obstruction of justice; that's a felony, perjury—messing with transcripts.

MARCH 23, 2024

Former ADA Josh Davila

Former ADA Josh Davila: I quit because DA Isidro "Chilo" Alaniz told me off, and he treats his employees like dirt.

Author: Did Perez ever say "mistrial" on the day you left? I was looking for that. I didn't find it.

Josh: I'm sorry. But to emphasize me leaving had nothing to do with the integrity or substance of the case. I prepared that case all by myself and DA Chilo just presented it. Me leaving had to do with the way he treats people who work for him. Several more prosecutors left in the weeks following. No one lasts with him.

Defense attorneys do that in every case. It's a common strategy.

I don't know. I wasn't there. I drove home.

Author: Did you ever pass by Juan David Ortiz's cell next to the court?

Josh: I did pass by and see him. There were 5 other guards there. I went downstairs to make sure the evidence was there and had to pass by where he was being held. I was escorted by a deputy.

You know Joel Perez's brother works for DA Chilo Alaniz?

Author: No, I didn't know Ortiz's attorney has his brother working for the DA.

I'm not against you. And I didn't blame you for leaving or for the results of the case. You leaving didn't affect the case—in my opinion. You didn't do anything wrong. You got tired of being disrespected—and left. It's that simple.

Josh: Yup!

Author: I believe you did a fantastic job at Ortiz's trial. You should run for DA when Chilo Alaniz retires. We need someone with balls to take over. We don't have anyone in Laredo.

Author: JD, did you know your attorney's brother worked for the DA?

JD: No, I didn't know. It's the first time I am hearing about this. Judge Hale's dad worked for the DA as an investigator; the dad retired before my case. Judge Hale is retiring after my case. His wife was the City Attorney for Laredo. Former ADA Maricela Jacaman quit after the Ronald Anthony Burgos-Aviles case. Former Josh Davila and Joaquin Rodriguez both quit during my case.

Ortiz's attorney, Joel Perez, faces a potential conflict of interest due to his brother's employment under District Attorney Isidro R. "Chilo" Alaniz. Albert Perez, a counselor for the Domestic Violence Unit, has dedicated nearly 24 years to assisting victims of domestic violence within Alaniz's jurisdiction. This connection raises questions about the integrity of Ortiz's case proceedings. Shouldn't this relationship have been disclosed during Ortiz's trial? Furthermore, the timing of Judge Hale's retirement following Ortiz's case prompts further speculation. Additionally, the resignation of Assistant District Attorney Maricela Jacaman after the Burgos-Aviles capital murder trial, another high-profile case, adds to the growing list of concerns surrounding the office's handling of these critical matters.

MARCH 31, 2024

Author: When did you speak to former ADA Josh Davila?

JD: It wasn't during my trial; it was a while back.

Author: Do you remember when ... what court date?

JD: I can't remember. It was when Josh Davila took over my case after former ADA Joaquin Rodriguez quit or was let go. Davila didn't go inside my cell. He asked me, "What is it that you want? Do you want *Life Without Parole*?"

Author: On another subject, I think your appeal is actually going to go through. It's more than likely going to end up at the Supreme Court with Justice Clarence Thomas, my favorite Supreme Court Justice.

JD: That's why Judge Hale probably left ... He didn't want to deal with my appeal.

JANUARY 13, 2024

Continuing Conversations with Juan David Ortiz

JD: I had a *mental breakdown*. They knew I was having one and were waiting for me to get another mental breakdown.

In the beginning, I wanted an attorney.

"I'm a disgrace to the blue." I never said that. I was green—border patrol. Why would I say blue?

The part where they were messing with my firearm in my truck is missing from the video. Where is the footage? They towed my truck to the substation. When we got to the substation, I said, "How did you guys get my truck? The keys are in my pocket." That part was not in any of the videos either.

I requested an attorney to Sgt. Noe Gonzalez when I got there. I told him, "When do I get an attorney?" Gonzalez told me, "They're going to read you your rights—right now."

There was no visible camera in the interrogation room. I didn't know I was being recorded. I was not given an attorney, even by asking for one. I was handcuffed and couldn't terminate the interview. I was not in the right state of mind.

I was taking the following medications: Paxil, Divalproex Sodium, Trazodone, and Gabapentin. I went to the VA because I had nightmares and couldn't sleep. I went to a 12-week program and all the appointments. I saw Dr. Shankar from Laredo VA and Dr. Patricia Amparan in San Antonio via Zoom at the VA branch clinic. They put me on all these medications ... and look at where I ended up. I'm not saying I did anything with this statement of "look at where I ended up." I was impeccable before.

Johnny Rodriguez (defense investigator) told me that the numbers were out of sequence, gaps in the statement videos, and the volume was up and down. The interrogation recording was manipulated. My attorney, Joel Perez, only saw me for 5 minutes before each hearing. They wanted me to sign the plea bargain; that's the only time they sat down with me. He told me, "That's the best that I can do."

At Webb County Jail—for 1 year and 3 months—I was left naked with a gown. They wouldn't give me a towel. I asked to be removed from that. I reported this to the Texas Commission on Jail Standards. Shane Sowell took me off 10 days later.

The reason I went to trial is because the statements were inadmissible. I was handcuffed to a chair. They tampered with the recording. The search was illegal—they put my firearm on the door panel.

Author: You were a runner ... right?

JD: I was in the Rock 'n' Roll San Antonio Marathon in 2011 and the LiveStrong Austin Marathon & Half Marathon in 2012. I was in track, cross country, and swimming—District Champion in swimming in high school. I was President of the Christian Club in high school ... I was literally a preacher.

Author: Did you give permission to Joey Tellez, your former attorney, to talk to the *Texas Monthly Magazine* about you?

JD: *The Texas Monthly Magazine* gave him questions and he only answered 3. He chose which questions he wanted to answer.

I was stationed at the Laredo North Station. When I worked in Cotulla Station as an agent, I lived in San Antonio, Texas. I saw people getting this information wrong, saying that I worked in Cotulla and lived in Laredo.

Both of my parents are U.S. citizens—all three of us are. I read somewhere that my parents were illegal.

During my trial, I prayed and fasted. I asked God to bless me with His presence; I kept praying, "With him at my right hand, I will not be shaken."— *Psalms 16:8 NIV*

At trial, during the last phone call, my wife said "God is in control." Judge Hale said "God is in control" too when he asked for that part to be repeated from the beginning. This is when I knew that God was giving me a sign that He was answering my prayers.

The evidence was inadmissible. I was an EMT in the BOAT Unit, Laredo Sector—Marine Operations. When I got here in TDCJ, I did 1,000 burpees, 3 days a week.

During my trial, the jury requested to go home ... and Judge Hale denied it. The jury made the decision shortly after. They were probably tired and wanted to get some rest. I wanted them to go home; it was a long day.

Author: Do you still have that Study Bible?

JD: My family sent me the New King James Version Study Bible. I watch sermons on the Pando app.

I was induced ... not coerced. I never got an attorney; I want the truth to be told. I told my defense team. It's the *fruit of the poisonous tree doctrine.*

Author: Did you ever have a psychological evaluation?

JD: I had a psychological exam 2 weeks before my trial. It was done by the prosecution. His name was Michael Junes or something like that. I told him what I told you. They focused on that I was a federal agent, calm and focused. He didn't ask me questions relating to my defense that I wasn't supposed to reveal to him; he was careful about that and what questions he asked me. The evidence was staged.

Author: Were you separated or getting a divorce?

JD: I was never getting a divorce.

Author: Was your house empty with no furniture?

JD: The house was not empty. It's hearsay.

I had a mental breakdown; the statements were inadmissible. I was squared away—it's a military term we use.

I was hired by the San Antonio Police Department. I was going to start—two days before—the government called me. I passed the SAPD background check and all the exams. It consisted of a psychological and lie detector exam. It was more intense than the government one. I also passed the federal background check—all at the same time. The SAPD background check is not easy to pass.

This is why I went to trial—I wanted the jury to determine if my rights were violated and wanted the truth to be revealed. Joaquin Rodriguez didn't file the controverting affidavit on time. A few weeks before my case, Joel Perez was working on his campaign to be elected as a judge and didn't pay attention to my case.

They lied to the jury, tampered with evidence, and violated my Miranda rights; the search of my truck was illegal. The evidence was inadmissible. That's why I took my case to trial. My attorneys are not stupid; they didn't take doctors or witnesses to testify at my trial. Due process was not followed. My Miranda rights were violated—and due process was not followed. I requested an attorney; they tampered with evidence in my truck and tampered with the video of my interrogation.

I was in El Poso (translation: the hole—segregation) for 1 year and 3 months at Webb County Jail. I was then moved to an 8-man cell—but we all had our cell. I'm now a P-7—non-aggressive. I was not in the right state of mind. All these issues I mentioned were removed from the transcripts. The search of my truck was illegal. Statements were altered ... promises were made—1st-degree murder.

They induced me, handcuffed me to a chair, and refused to get me an attorney. The prosecutor was present, knew about bargaining, and that I asked for an attorney. I told all of my defense team. Johnny Rodriguez told me the numbers were out of sequence and there were time gaps in the interrogation video. Those were his exact words. He told Joel Perez about this. It was quid pro quo and bargaining. That's a rogue sheriff and prosecutor.

JANUARY 14, 2024

JD: During my interrogation with Federico Calderon and EJ Salinas, I stated that Investigator David Liendo, who works for Webb County Sheriff's Office, would pick up prostitutes on San Bernardo Ave. Liendo was fired from Webb County for crashing a unit about one year after my arrest. David Liendo was involved in my case—but he would pick up prostitutes.

This segment about Liendo was missing. Why didn't the jury see that? Liendo was trying to get into the constable's office to get a job. On the night of my arrest, we talked about David Liendo being involved with my case. David Liendo booked me at Webb County Jail. I told all this to Johnny Rodriguez, the defense investigator.

Author: David Liendo executed and signed your search warrants (except for the last one), but he was also Erika Peña's client—a regular. Isn't that a conflict of interest?

JD: How do I know this? Erika Peña told me that Liendo is a client and that he's a regular.

I wanted the jury to consider that I was induced, asked for an attorney, refused to sign, and bargaining occurred. I also wanted the jury to consider the truck. I was parked and legally established ownership of the truck. Bail-out doesn't apply to my case. The truck was legally parked—I wasn't escaping with the truck. They went into the truck and took out the gun—and they inserted a magazine. They put it in the driver's door panel, took a picture, and used it as evidence—tampering with evidence.

Was the statement voluntary? They made promises—they promised first-degree murder. I was induced. They originally charged me with first-degree murder. My firearm was in the glove compartment. The glove compartment was locked, and my firearm was not loaded. My truck was seized. Hector Rodriguez worked at the Sheriff's Office—and was having sex with inmates. One of the female inmates made an outcry.

The biggest problem is the truck. Was the truck information valid? It was the *fruit of the poisonous tree*. I also was not given an attorney. I requested a lawyer 3 times. Ugarte and EJ Salinas were taking pictures of my truck. They skipped over the part in the video where they tampered with the truck. They knowingly and willingly tampered with evidence.

JANUARY 15, 2024

Author: I noticed that in the video, Calderon was the one who started making all these derogatory remarks about the victims. He was leading you.

JD: Thank you ... I'm glad you noticed. After a while, I started repeating what he was saying.

Author: You were an intel supervisor, right?

JD: My job title was Supervisory Border Patrol Agent (SBPA) detailed to the South Texas Border Intelligent Center (BIC) within the Laredo Sector Operations Center. I was a tenured supervisor stationed at the Laredo North Station; I was permanent—SBPA.

Author: If they told you that you had to go fight Hamas in Israel right now, and if you made it back, you would be free ... would you go?

JD: YES ...

JD: Calderon shook his head ... yes ... that he knew—when I told him that I had my firearm locked in the glove compartment, during my interrogation—which was not shown to the jury and was removed from the video.

JD: I was very proud of my credit score.

Author: What was your score?

JD: From my memory, it was 812 or 813. I don't know the exact number.

Author: That's a high score.

Author: So ... were you in love with any of the women?

JD: I was not going to leave my wife and family for anyone ... or was falling in love with any woman. I had conversations ... and I was just there ... but I wasn't in love or liking anyone. I wasn't having any relationships or obsessed with anyone. It's all hearsay.

Author: I know ... as it is, it's so hard to fall in love, get attached, or feel anything for anyone these days. I can't even fall asleep.

Author: Did you ever tell Erika Peña that you wanted to start a new life with her or have a future with her?

JD: That was her fantasy, not mine. I love my wife. I didn't want a future or life with her.

Ortiz categorically refutes any inclination toward establishing a personal relationship with Erika Peña, firmly maintaining that their interactions were strictly professional. He contends that she was merely a client and any insinuation of a personal connection stemmed solely from her own imagination, entirely misaligned with his true intentions. His allegiance remains steadfastly with his wife, to whom he has been devoted for nearly two decades, a duration encompassing half of his life.

JD: I don't have anything against Erika Peña. I'm not mad at her or anything. I know she had to lie and testify against me ... because the prosecution told her to do it. Some of the statements she made were not true. I never threw her phone out the window. She left her phone in my truck ... and I didn't know what to do with it. I went to her house to drop off her phone ... but they said she wasn't living there; they said she was living in a hotel.

JD: I knew where she lived ... because she would ask me to drop her off there. Was I a regular? Yes ... but 5 times is too many. I didn't have time; I was too busy working—I was a supervisor—and I had a family. I hope she gets the help she needs. I feel bad for her—because she was used and coached by the prosecution on what to say in court. She even said in court that she liked me and considered me a friend; she said that I was good to her and would buy her food. I told her—before that she could get better and do something with herself ... since she knew how to have a conversation.

Author: I want to lose weight—but I like to eat chips and cookies.

JD: Me too ... that's all I eat ... junk food. I eat these Mexican (Marias) cookies with coffee. I have to eat them with my coffee in the morning.

Author: OMG ... those are my favorite cookies too. I like plain ones. They are super good and simple. My mother usually gets me some when she goes to the store.

JD: Yes ... I eat the plain ones too.

JANUARY 16-18, 2024

Author: Where did you hang out?

JD: I was always at the public library ... the main one.

Author: I never saw you there—but I didn't go as much as I should have gone.

JD: Joel Perez sent your emails to my wife and my family.

Author: Joel Perez told me to send him any emails for you and that he would relay them to you.

JD: He also said that you would send him naughty pics once in a while.

Author: I don't remember ever sending him any nudes. The pics I sent him, with clothes, were for you.

JD: I was a Collateral Intelligence Agent in Cotulla from 2009-2015, and attended the Detecting Deception and Eliminating Responses (DDER) in Glynco, Georgia. They made a book about this.

JD: I had my house custom-built.

Author: Oh, wow. I thought you bought it like that—the last house you had before your arrest.

JD: Captain Magana did everything to keep me from speaking to you.

Author: I don't even know who that guy is. The more they forbid something, the more you want it. It's reverse psychology.

JD: I lived in La Bota Ranch in a house—before.

Author: I didn't know.

JD: I was a "librarian" at Webb County Jail, thanks to all the books you sent me. Since I came out in the media a lot, the other inmates came to ask me to borrow a book. They all knew me as the library guy. I was the only one with many books.

Author: Well, they were able to keep all the books and the books kept you busy. They should be thankful … LOL!

JD: This chick from another state sent me a letter on pink paper. It got rejected and sent back to her after I paid for the stamp. She was trying to be all personal. Another guy wrote me a letter that he wanted to write a book about me and that I was the only serial killer with the most education—after Ted Bundy. He said he knew I was trying to help. All the media letters I get—say the same thing to me: "We want to hear your side of the story."

JD: I was in the Laredo Sector—Marine Operations Unit—where I was a crew member in the BOAT Unit.

JD: Hearing my kids and my wife talk about God in the phone call was overwhelming for me. That's when I started to cry and put a tissue over my face—during my trial.

JANUARY 23, 2024

JD: *50 Shades of Grey* was my most popular book that all the other inmates would borrow and bring back ... they would check it out like a library. They would see me in the news and knew who I was ... so they would come borrow books from me. They all knew I had a lot of books.

JD: Two Webb County Jail officers would have sex—during work hours—in a space/room. The officer is not working there anymore.

JD: Lt. Sara Elizondo said she didn't know where my court attire was at. They found it; my name and picture were on it. On October 17, 2022, the night of my transfer to Bexar County Jail, Deputy Roque brought me another suit that wasn't mine. Commander Jose Hernandez, Jail Administrator, was present.

JD: Officer Garcin and Sort Commander transferred me to Bexar County Jail. Johnny Rodriguez (investigator for the defense) went to Bexar County Jail to see my property—to get my suits—to take them to get ironed. They took my suit and replaced it with shorts and another inmate's suit. Webb County Sheriff's Officers stole my expensive suits that I wore to work, my Tony Lama boots, shirts, and ties. Tony Lama boots aren't cheap; they cost $300-$500. My relatives had to go buy me new suits that same day. When they searched my home, they stole my master's degree ring with diamonds on it. My master's degree is very important to me; it's my most valuable achievement.

JANUARY 24, 2024

Author: It's shameful how Webb County Sheriff's Department officers are money-hungry thieves. I don't understand what a gold ring with diamonds on it has anything to do with your case. This is not legal or ethical. It's an abuse of power ... color of law. It's disgusting how they treat a war veteran with PTSD—who was not in the right state of mind and has TBI (Traumatic brain injury).

JD: I fell off my bike, hit my head, was bleeding, had a concussion, and stitches were needed on base in Okinawa, Japan—when I was deployed there. That was one of my concussions. Mount Fuji was a field op in mainland Japan.

JD: I remember when you sent a priest to check on me when I was at Webb County Jail. I was telling Burgos that a priest came to visit me and I'm not even Catholic.

Author: LOL ...

JD: They didn't let me cut my nails at Webb County Jail. And when they finally did, they passed the same nail clipper to all the inmates.

Author: That's so unsanitary.

JD: I know.

JD: My favorite song is "Rebel Yell" by Billy Idol. I would jam out to it in my truck. Listen to the lyrics; remember me when you hear this song.

"In the midnight hour, she cried more, more, more, more

With a rebel yell she cried more, more, more

In the midnight hour, babe, more, more, more

With a rebel yell more, more, more

More, more, more!"—Billy Idol

Author: That's one of my favorite songs too—because it came out in *American Horror Story (AHS)*. "AHS 1984: Montana's Midnight Manerobics" scene is hilarious. They made Richard Ramirez look gay. He would be mad if he saw it. LOL …

JD: No, I have never seen or heard of *American Horror Story*.

Author: I can't believe you never heard of *American Horror Story*.

JD: They should have free phone calls in Texas. They have that in California; they don't charge inmates to make calls. You should start that here.

Author: A petition needs to be started; all the families who can't afford the phone calls would benefit from this; they are the ones who get stuck paying the bill. The inmates would be in a better state of mind; that's how they stay sane—by having contact with the outside world. This would make correctional officers' lives easier at work. The governor needs to sign it here in Texas. Newsom signed it in California. They should at least offer an unlimited plan of $50 a month. It would be offered in TDCJ and county jails. They should include federal prisons too.

FEBRUARY 9, 2024

Author: Did Webb County Jail staff mistreat you when you were there?

JD: They treated me and Burgos inhumanely. They didn't want to give Burgos a toothbrush.

FEBRUARY 18, 2024

JD: Did you watch *20/20*?

Author: No—

JD: Ranger EJ Salinas said he saw the devil come out of me in the show *20/20*.

Author: Yet, he stated under oath that you were perfectly fine to continue the interrogation— since he studies mannerisms. Which one is it? He can't have it both ways; he is contradicting himself. Salinas is admitting on a national television show that something was wrong with you that night—and you were not perfectly normal. His ego will come back to haunt him when this case goes to the Supreme Court for—violating your right to an attorney when you asked for one— three times, and you were denied and ignored.

JD: The DA came out on *Dateline* and *20/20* saying that he saw the confession in the other room. So—that means he was watching me ask for an attorney 3 times— and getting offered deals, quid pro quo.

JD: My attorney—Raymond Fuchs told me, "Consider how it's going to make us look that you don't take the deal—of taking the death penalty off the table." Raymond Fuchs said, "Jesus doesn't show up to trials." He tried to take away my faith. My faith was what kept me going. Joel Perez was concerned about the comments being made online during the trial; he was keeping track of them.

Author: He should have focused solely on the case. It's sad that you had no defense and that your attorneys were more worried about how they look—rather than your mental health— and where and how you will spend the rest of your life. They threw you in a box—with no consideration that you were a war veteran with PTSD—who needed state hospital type of treatment to get better.

JD: Johnny Rodriguez, defense investigator, was denied to see me at Webb County Jail—even after showing his credentials. He was part of my defense team; he wanted to talk to me about my case.

Author: So ... the Webb County Sheriff's Office blocked your defense ...

JD: In 2022, after I had met with Dr. Crowder and Dr. De La Torre, Danielle Cantu went to Webb County Jail to do a competency exam on me; she works for Dr. De La Torre. The test consisted of drawing stuff and motor skills. She needed Wi-Fi to test me on a part—that needed to be done on her tablet—and to complete the test. Cantu asked Jose Hernandez, the jail administrator, who said "No!" The psychological exam was not completed—because Jose Hernandez REFUSED!

Author: That constitutes interference and obstruction of your due process. It is perplexing why the Webb County Sheriff's Office displayed such hostile and abusive behavior towards you. Their duty does not encompass judgment of individuals; rather, it pertains to ensuring safety and well-being. They ought to reconsider their career choices and consider enrolling in anger management courses. Their actions warrant reporting to the Department of Justice. Section 242 of Title 18 stipulates that it is unlawful for individuals acting under the color of law to deliberately deprive someone of their rights or privileges protected by the Constitution or U.S. laws. Those acting under the color of law under this provision include law enforcement officers and prison guards. The offense carries penalties ranging up to a life sentence, which could be cited in your appeal. Had Joel Perez instituted a gag order on your case similar to Eddie Peña's action in the Burgos case, the prosecution and Sheriff's Office would have been prevented from engaging with the media to further tarnish your reputation. This is where opportunists exploited the situation to gain fleeting fame.

Author: You don't seem to feel guilty or act guilty ... as if you feel you didn't do anything wrong—and it was the pills.

JD: Yeah ...

CHAPTER 7
INVISIBLE WAR SCARS

Juan David Ortiz can be classified as a mission-oriented killer. Individuals who fall into this category often justify their homicidal actions as a means of "purifying" society by eliminating those they deem undesirable, including the homeless, ex-convicts, homosexuals, drug users, prostitutes, or individuals of different ethnicities or religions. Despite their heinous acts, these killers are typically not psychotic.

Cultural references, such as the television series *Dexter*, exemplify mission-oriented killers. Moreover, real-life examples include those who target specific groups, such as prostitutes or homosexuals. The overarching aim of such individuals is the complete eradication of the targeted group from society, as infamously illustrated by the Zodiac Killer.

— FBI

"Profiles in Terror: The Serial Murderer," R. M. Holmes (1989) delineates various typologies of serial killers, providing a nuanced understanding of their motivations and behavioral patterns. Holmes identifies three primary categories: mission-oriented, hedonistic, and power/control-oriented killers. The mission-oriented killer seeks to eradicate a specific group, such as prostitutes or women, whom they deem undesirable. The hedonistic killer, by contrast, derives pleasure from the act of killing itself. Lastly, the power/control-oriented killer gains satisfaction from dominating and controlling a helpless victim.

Holmes further elucidates that, despite these typological differences, serial killers generally share certain demographic and behavioral characteristics. Typically, they are white males aged between 25 and 34 years. They often possess charismatic and intelligent traits, facilitating their ability to engage with victims. Mobility is a common feature among them, and they frequently commit murders that involve direct contact with their victims. While their initial murders may be meticulously premeditated, subsequent killings often devolve into acts of panic or frenzy. Many of these individuals have histories of childhood abuse and substance abuse.

This framework is particularly pertinent when examining the case of Juan David Ortiz, a former Border Patrol agent accused of being a serial killer. Ortiz's profile aligns with Holmes' general characterization: he is a male within the specified age range, and his alleged victims were individuals he targeted as part of a mission-oriented agenda. Ortiz reportedly murdered several women whom he viewed as societal outcasts, consistent with the mission-oriented type described by Holmes. Additionally, Ortiz's method of operation—engaging directly with his victims and exhibiting an escalating pattern of violence—corresponds with the behavioral patterns identified by Holmes.

MISSION-ORIENTED KILLER

A mission-oriented serial killer consciously adopts a goal to eliminate a specific identifiable group of individuals. This type of killer does not experience auditory or visual hallucinations but independently determines that it is his responsibility to eradicate a group of people deemed "undesirable" or unfit to coexist with others in society.

Juan David Ortiz exemplifies such a killer. Recently, he was involved in the murder of four women, all of whom were prostitutes. Their frequentation of local nightspots signaled their availability for personal gain through sexual transactions. Ortiz justified his actions as a means to cleanse his community of prostitutes. During his interrogation, Ortiz expressed awareness of his crimes and took pride in what he perceived as a significant service to his community.

—*R. M. Holmes*

Juan David Ortiz, a mission-oriented serial murderer, had a self-imposed duty to rid the world of an unworthy group of people. His actions stemmed from a self-imposed obligation to eliminate what he perceived as an undeserving segment of society. This victim group could encompass individuals such as prostitutes, women, Catholics, or any other demographic he deemed unfit to coexist with morally upright citizens. Ortiz exhibited traits that were comparable to those of either an organized nonsocial or a disorganized asocial personality type. He actively engaged with the real world in his daily interactions.

Often, upon his arrest, neighbors expressed disbelief that such a person could be responsible for the deaths of numerous individuals.

—*R. M. Holmes*

In the context of Ortiz, his actions were driven by a mission to eliminate all sex workers in Laredo, Texas. Questions arise regarding the role of medication, specifically Paxil, which Ortiz consumed. Would this tragedy have unfolded differently if Ortiz had not taken Paxil? The VA's practice of administering uniform medication to PTSD veterans, regardless of individual differences, raises concerns about its effectiveness and impact on individuals like Ortiz.

Can Ortiz achieve normalcy again? Is there a viable solution for Ortiz and others similar to him? Rehabilitation remains a pivotal consideration. Preventing such tragedies hinges significantly on addressing mental health issues on both sides—the perpetrator and the victims. Ortiz, a veteran grappling with PTSD, should have received tailored medication that did not exacerbate his condition. Meanwhile, victims required interventions encompassing drug rehabilitation, HIV, and Hepatitis C treatment to curtail community spread.

Comparisons to COVID-19 underscore the importance of proactive measures against viruses, yet legal responses to drug-related offenses must evolve beyond punitive measures. Redirecting cases to rehabilitation centers instead of prisons offers a path to recovery, fostering familial reintegration and improved quality of life.

The presence of victims in precarious situations underscores systemic failures, urging law enforcement to enforce anti-prostitution laws while guiding individuals toward rehabilitation centers instead of criminal penalties. Human trafficking compounds these issues, necessitating stricter legal measures to protect vulnerable populations.

Laredo's urgent need for drug rehabilitation and mental health facilities cannot be overstated. Effective governance, particularly in downtown and San Bernardo Avenue districts, is crucial in addressing homelessness, addiction, and broader community welfare issues. Investing in facilities like the Old Mercy Hospital could provide vital resources to uplift vulnerable populations, countering the superficial gestures of indifferent elites.

Ultimately, systemic change requires informed electoral choices and substantial community investment in healthcare infrastructure. Only then can Laredo begin to comprehensively address its pressing social challenges and safeguard its most vulnerable residents.

"Insanity is doing the same thing over and over and expecting different results."

—*Albert Einstein*

To address the pressing issues facing our city, we urgently need new leadership that prioritizes transparency and accountability in how taxpayer money is allocated. Investing in the rehabilitation and well-being of our homeless population should be a moral imperative, reflecting our shared humanity.

In the neurology of a normal individual, the left side of the brain typically exhibits higher activity compared to the right side. However, in the brains of serial killers, there is often reduced activity in the prefrontal cortex. This area plays a crucial role in personality traits and cognitive functions such as empathy, judgment, and planning. This neurological difference contributes to a distinct thought process in serial killers, diverging significantly from that of the average person.

Understanding these neurological distinctions underscores the complex nature of criminal behavior and the importance of comprehensive approaches to mental health and rehabilitation. Effective leadership must prioritize these issues to foster a safer and more compassionate community for all residents.

THE BRAIN

Dr. Daniel Amen stated, "The brains of murderers typically exhibit unhealthy characteristics. Brain SPECT imaging, a technology measuring blood flow and brain activity, reveals three patterns: regions with healthy activity, excessive activity, and deficient activity. While SSRIs, the most commonly prescribed antidepressants, are generally safe, they may heighten impulsivity and provoke uncharacteristic behaviors in individuals with diminished activity in specific brain regions. Positioned behind the eyes and below the temples, the temporal lobes frequently correlate with acts of assault, murder, rape, arson, and other criminal behaviors. Further scientific inquiry supports the link between temporal lobe anomalies and heightened aggression and violence."

Regarding Juan David Ortiz, the information from Dr. Daniel Amen's research suggests that individuals with abnormalities in the temporal lobes, often linked to increased aggression and violent tendencies, might be more prone to committing serious crimes such as those allegedly committed by Juan David Ortiz.

A burgeoning corpus of neuroimaging research, as evidenced by a 2020 study in the *International Journal of Molecular Sciences* and a 2019 study in *The American Journal of Psychiatry*, indicates that brain imaging holds promise in predicting favorable responses to antidepressant treatments among patients. The role of the brain in decision-making is crucial. Current scientific findings underscore the critical influence of the brain on real-time behavior and emphasize its significance in judicial sentencing.

—*Dr. Daniel Amen*

Regarding Juan David Ortiz, this information could relate by highlighting the potential implications of neuroscientific evidence in cases involving behavior and decision-making. Ortiz's actions and their judicial implications could be analyzed in light of how brain imaging research contributes to understanding behavior and its legal ramifications.

In considering the case of Juan David Ortiz, the question arises: What if our society shifted from merely incarcerating troubled individuals in stressful environments to actively evaluating and treating their underlying brain health issues? Dr. Daniel Amen, drawing on over three decades of experience at Amen Clinics, suggests that such a shift could lead to significant societal benefits. By improving brain health through proactive treatment, individuals, including violent offenders reintegrating into society, stand a better chance of becoming productive contributors, supporting themselves, and contributing to tax revenues.

—Dr. Daniel Amen

According to Dr. Daniel Amen, "A society should be judged not by how it treats its outstanding citizens, but by how it treats its criminals." He advocates for a comprehensive approach that includes the use of Single-Photon Emission Computed Tomography (SPECT) imaging to assess and treat criminal behavior beyond traditional crime and punishment paradigms. SPECT imaging, a nuclear imaging technique employing a radioactive tracer and specialized cameras, provides detailed 3D images of bodily organs, tissues, and bones.

—Dr. Daniel Amen

Individual responses to PTSD vary significantly. Juan David Ortiz exemplifies a case where combat-related PTSD, stemming from his military service, plays a pivotal role. Ortiz, a veteran, exhibited heightened irritability and anger management issues. Unlike individuals without his background, the act of killing did not evoke the same psychological impact due to his training, where violence was a problem-solving method. PTSD operates cognate to a lit stick of dynamite with a progressively shortening fuse, leading to explosive outcomes. It is crucial to note that PTSD severity varies among veterans, emphasizing the need to avoid generalizations. While deployment marked one phase, reintegrating into civilian life proves arduous. Seeking a SPECT scan by Dr. Amen could offer insights into Ortiz's brain activity, guiding potential rehabilitation efforts. Ortiz's struggles with PTSD, coupled with panic attacks and paranoia exacerbated by alcohol and medication misuse, underscore the complexity of his situation.

Movie Scene from *No Man of God*

FBI Analyst Bill Hagmaier: We're compiling a series of interviews to try to find common threads in the way people think. We find it very helpful to understand what childhood was like for people in your situation—what triggers their aggression? What makes them angry?

Ted Bundy: My situation—

BH: Your situation is unique in that you also have, from what I understand, an interest in the psychology of serial murders ...

TB: I do. Yes ... you mean that Green River thing? It's a really interesting case. I don't have access to everything, but I started to piece some things together.

BH: —and that thought process is why I wanted to speak to you.

TB: No ... it isn't—

BH: It's purely academic ...

TB: I know what this is ... oh, you FBI guys—you're all the same. You think you're better than me—and you've got the biggest brain in the room.

BH: I just want to recruit you to help me see if we're going down the right road on this. Are we asking the right questions? Are we looking at the right people? I'm not here looking for evidence ... I'm looking for understanding. I don't know what you know—I don't see what you see. I don't hear what you hear—

TB: ... you really think Playboy makes people do these things?

BH: —no ...

TB: ... neither do I ...

BH: I'll tell you what the real bad pornography is ... the marriage of pleasure with the thrill of control—

"The author posits, 'I am here in pursuit of understanding, striving to comprehend your perspective and unique mindset. By cultivating a more profound awareness, we might avert the recurrence of such tragedies. In this instance, recidivism is not the desired outcome. I do not perceive the world as you do.'"

The dialogue from the movie *No Man of God* between FBI Analyst Bill Hagmaier and Ted Bundy explores the psychological insights into serial murder. It delves into understanding the motivations and thought processes of individuals like Bundy who commit such crimes. This relates to Juan David Ortiz, a former Border Patrol agent charged with murdering multiple women in Texas, as both cases involve understanding the mindset and motives of serial killers to potentially prevent similar tragedies.

I believe Ortiz should be deployed to Israel to combat Hamas; he is deeply religious and possesses formidable combat skills. As a military veteran, Ortiz's expertise should be utilized effectively. His deployment could mirror the narrative of the movie *Suicide Squad*, reminiscent of Harley Quinn's role in combat.

The violence perpetrated by Hamas is shocking. They have horrifically murdered 40 infants through beheading and burning, alongside the brutalization, rape, and murder of women. The widespread pro-Hamas demonstrations indicate a disturbing acceptance of violence against Jewish communities. Witnessing these events unfold is deeply troubling. It appears that violence is increasingly normalized, tolerated out of fear of reprisal from the radical left's cancel culture.

I adamantly oppose the genocide of Israel. Therefore, hearing about Ortiz's past as a serial killer does not surprise me. Recent events reflect widespread brutality. The conflict in Israel has endured for 2,000 years, dating back to biblical times. Amidst the media frenzy over Juan David Ortiz and the pursuit of fleeting fame, I am focused on studying his case.

FEBRUARY 11, 2024

JD: I saw a psychiatrist sent by the defense and paid for by the court—on May 4, 2022. His name is Dr. Jaye D. Crowder. His office is located in Dallas, Texas. He was accompanied by Dr. John De La Torre and Dr. Jayna M. Mercado from San Antonio, Texas. Dr. Mercado is a neuropsychologist.

I told Dr. Crowder the following:

You didn't talk to me on the night of my arrest, so you could have seen the condition that I was in. You talk to me 4 years later after the medication is out of my system. Look at the interrogation video. Those pills did something to me. I didn't understand that at the time. I was not in the right state of mind. I was taking medication. I was following Dr.'s orders by taking all my medication. I thought I had done something good by going to the doctor to get help, so that's why I kept taking my medication. The VA put me on 8 pills per day. I saw things in my truck. I was hearing things at the time. I smelled different things; I smelled gas. I had visual hallucinations. At the time, I thought I was doing something good for Laredo. I was cleaning the streets. I didn't think I was doing something bad. That was my state of mind at that time.

I was going to work like I normally do because I didn't believe I was doing something wrong. The pills made me do things that were out of my character with unusual behavior. I had an impeccable record, married to one woman, and had kids with the same woman. No, I don't have any diseases—HIV and STDs. For those who said that I was perfectly fine, my behavior was not normal. It's like being under the influence and having something control you—where you are not your normal self. If I was perfectly normal, why did Webb County Jail have me in a gown in a padded room for 10 days after my arrest? They had me naked in a gown for more than a year. The real—normal JD likes women who are highly educated and attractive.

Author: If you thought you were doing something wrong, you would have colored your hair blonde, taken all your money, and ran to Mexico like Scott Peterson. Instead, you kept going like *The Terminator*. That's not normal.

JD: I was also suicidal. I thought that by taking the pills and following doctor's orders, I was going to get the help I needed. I was doing something good by going to the doctor to get help.

Federico Calderon and EJ Salinas denied me my medication after I asked for it. They saw me cry when they mentioned my family, so they knew my soft spot and where to get me. They got me in my soft spot, my family.

Elizabeth Harvey, mitigation specialist, said, "You have a temporary insanity defense." As per the legal definition, at the time of the commission, I thought I was doing something good for Laredo and not something wrong—at the time of the arrest.

Dr. De La Torre was asking me questions that the media had stated about me. He used news articles. I told him he was proving my point that I wasn't going to get a fair trial—due to what the media was saying about me. He was being biased against me—himself. I never spoke to the media ... so they know nothing about me. They made me out to be a vigilante.

As for the legal aspect of my case, my Miranda rights were violated by Federico Calderon and EJ Salinas. They conducted an illegal search. They perjured themselves under oath when they said that I never asked for an attorney. Dr. Crowder asked me why my case was not being tried at the federal level. I told him that the DA and Sheriff are elected officials. The DA knows that the evidence used against me will not stand at the federal level, and that's why they are keeping it at the state level, not the federal level.

I was handcuffed to a chair. I could not terminate the interrogation. I asked for an attorney 3 times, and they denied me an attorney. They tampered with the inside of my truck by moving the firearm to the door panel, after taking it out of the glove compartment. They put a magazine in the firearm.

The State not pursuing the death penalty—changed everything. My insanity defense and all the hard work done by Dr. Crowder, Elizabeth Harvey, and Johnny Rodriguez went out the window. My PTSD diagnosis was not brought up. Joel Perez said, "We got victory, and that's it." He told me I had two choices: life or death—that's all. His strategy was to object to everything in my trial ... so I could use it for my appeal. He kept his word—and that's what he did. He was working on his campaign to be judge for a year, instead of working my case.

Author: He performed inadequately and showed disregard for your mental health. He failed to vigorously advocate for your placement in a state hospital for necessary mental health treatment, allowing you to be incarcerated without adequate support. This constitutes ineffective counsel for your appeal. He neglected to disclose crucial information that could have been beneficial, opting instead to undermine your case.

JD: I went to trial because I wanted my truth to come out and be presented to the jury—the violation of my Miranda rights, my mental health, and my state of mind.

It was a combination of alcohol, pills, stress, and not being able to sleep. I would go for days without sleeping. I thought I was doing something good by taking my pills and following doctor's orders. The doctor at the VA knew I had an alcohol problem—and he still gave me Paxil pills and the rest of the medications.

Author: Paxil medication needs to be banned. Imagine all the other people who have been victims of this Paxil—dangerous medication. That VA doctor should be held liable for giving you Paxil medication. Had he not given you Paxil—you wouldn't have done what you did and been where you are at ... today. That doctor should have done his research on Paxil pills. He basically drugged you and made you—go into zombie mode. That guy that night is not the real you—JD.

JD: This is why I came to you to state my truth and not all the other media and people who contacted me. I feel comfortable with you and you went to all my hearings.

Author: "On November 28, 2022, during the first day of your trial, Erika Peña testified under oath that she lacked the expertise to assess your mental state for conditions such as depression, suicidal tendencies, or anxiety. At the time, she was a heroin-influenced sex worker, without the qualifications of a medical doctor or trained psychiatrist.

During your trial, EJ Salinas justified his continued interrogation based on his knowledge of your occupation and studied mannerisms, asserting you exhibited no signs of mental illness. However, Ranger Salinas, lacking medical or psychiatric credentials, is not qualified to diagnose mental health conditions.

Calderon and Salinas acted under the color of law when they violated your constitutional rights by unlawfully searching your vehicle and depriving you of legal counsel. This conduct constitutes a crime under federal law, which prohibits individuals acting under color of law from willfully depriving others of rights guaranteed by the U.S. Constitution and laws. Qualified immunity does not shield officials who violate clearly established statutory or constitutional rights that a reasonable person would recognize."

JD: Elizabeth Harvey told me that I was insane at that moment. She was a mitigation specialist who was part of my legal team. I told all this to my legal defense team.

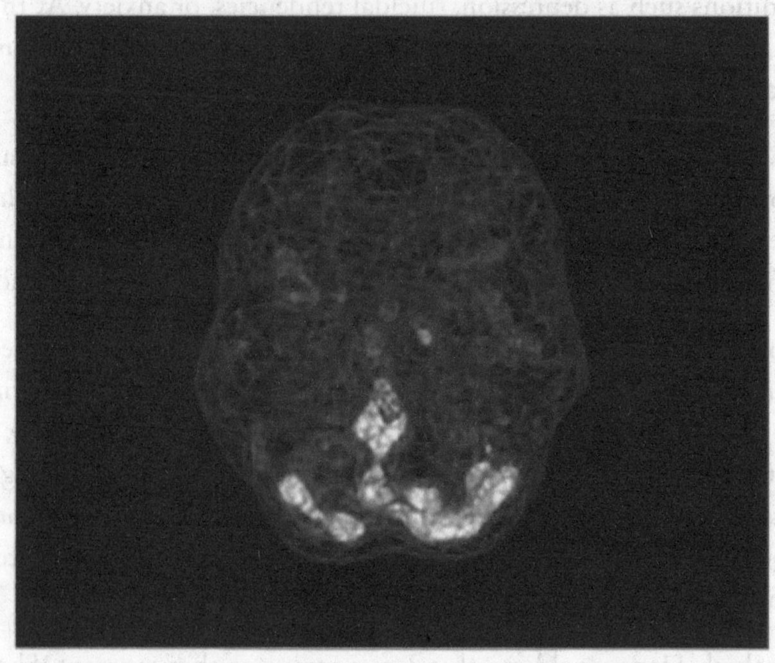

Healthy Brain Scan

Dr. Daniel Amen from Amen Clinics—single-photon emission computerized tomography (SPECT) scan from a Healthy Brain. *Courtesy of Dr. Daniel Amen*

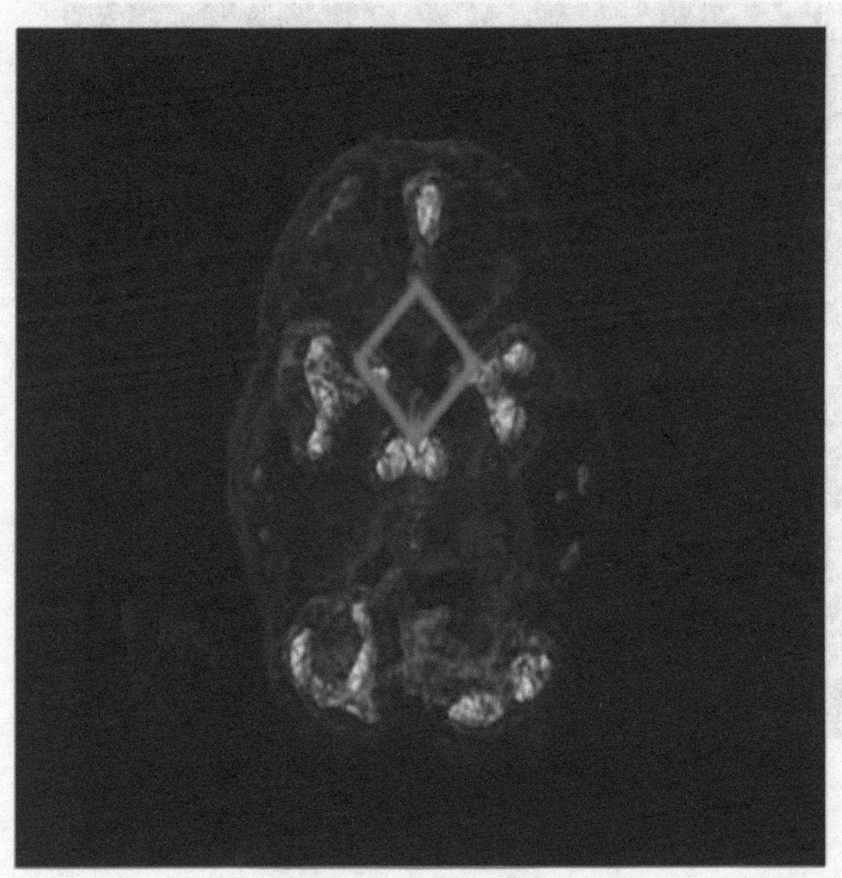

Dr. Daniel Amen—from Amen Clinics—PTSD Brain (SPECT) scan. *Courtesy of Dr. Daniel Amen*

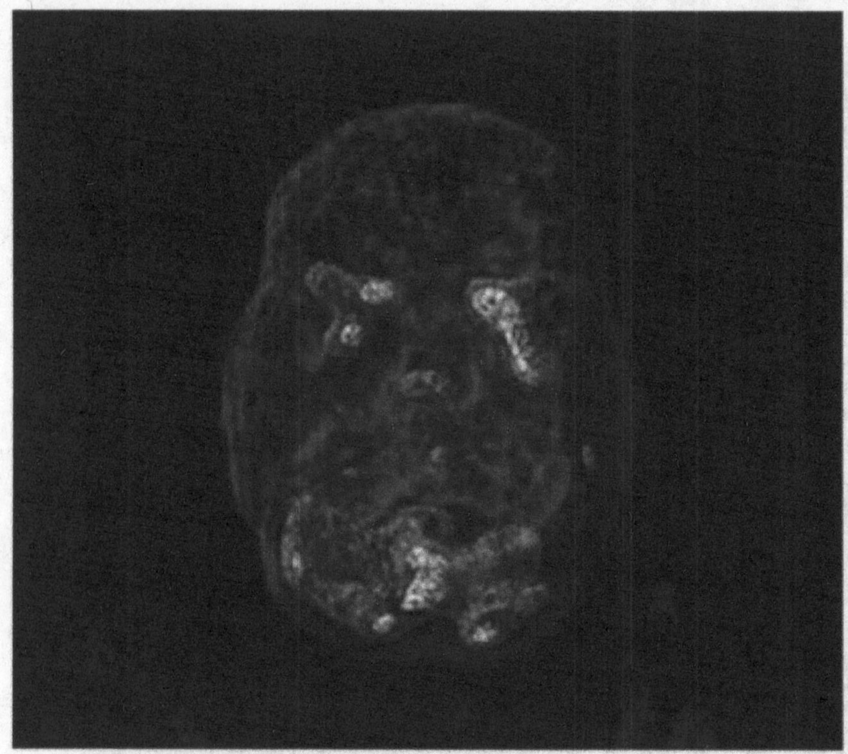

Dr. Daniel Amen—from Amen Clinics—Panic Disorder Brain (SPECT) scan. *Courtesy of Dr. Daniel Amen*

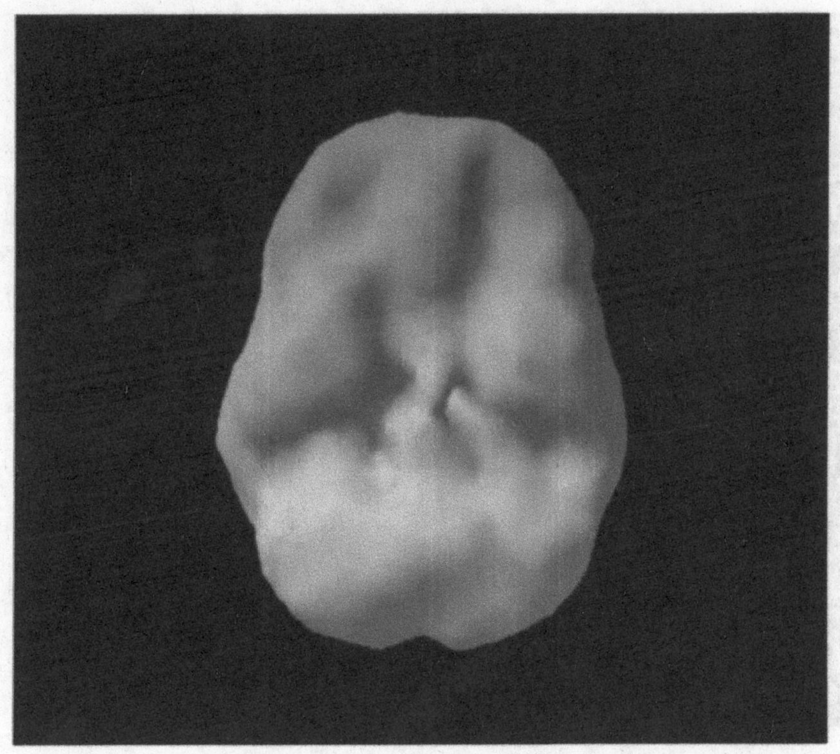

Dr. Daniel Amen—from Amen Clinics—Healthy (SPECT) scan. *Courtesy of Dr. Daniel Amen*

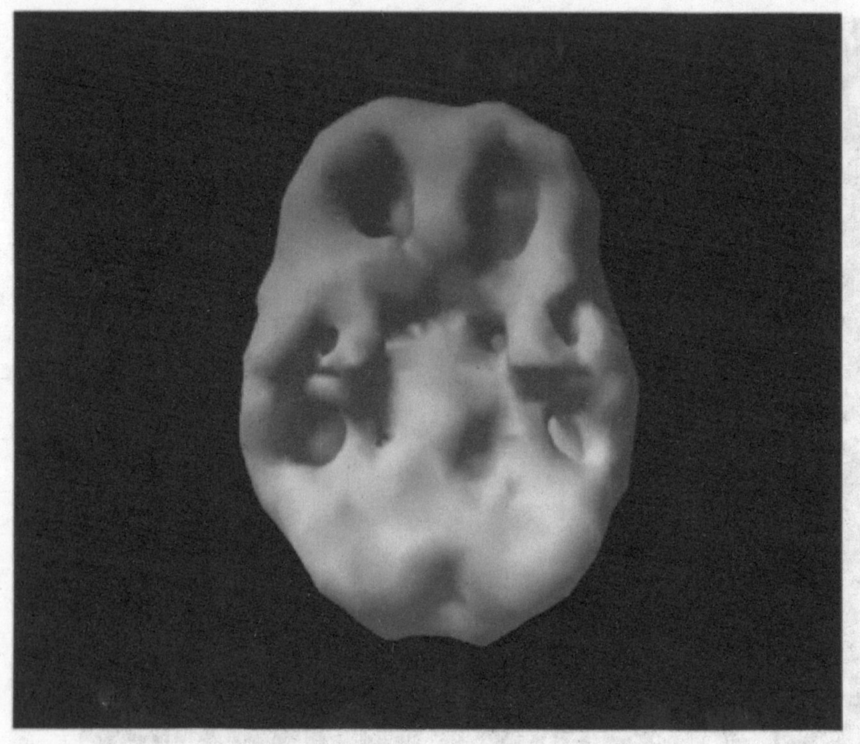

Dr. Daniel Amen—from Amen Clinics—Suicidal Brain (SPECT) scan. *Courtesy of Dr. Daniel Amen*

CHAPTER 8
THE LAW

HIV and STDs

Federico Calderon: All the victims were HIV positive and had Hepatitis C. I'm concerned about your wife. Tell your wife to get checked.

Juan David Ortiz: She is good to go.

Calderon reported that all the victims had tested positive for HIV and were diagnosed with Hepatitis C. Concerning Juan David Ortiz, he was advised about his wife's health, prompting the recommendation for her to undergo testing.

Juan David Ortiz responded affirmatively regarding his wife's current health status.

Texas lacks specific criminal statutes addressing the intentional transmission of sexually transmitted diseases (STDs). Nevertheless, individuals may face prosecution under Texas assault laws for transmitting HIV or other STDs. In certain instances, prosecutors may pursue charges of assault with a deadly weapon or attempted murder.

Assault involves the intentional, knowing, or reckless infliction of bodily injury upon another person, encompassing physical pain, physical illness, or any impairment of physical condition. By this definition, knowingly transmitting an STD to a sexual partner could constitute bodily injury. A conviction for assault results in a class A misdemeanor penalty, carrying a sentence of up to one year in jail and a fine of $4,000.

If the transmission leads to "serious bodily injury," defined as posing a substantial risk of death, the offense escalates to aggravated assault, a second-degree felony punishable by imprisonment for 2 to 20 years. Although most STDs do not typically present a risk of death, Texas courts recognize HIV as a fatal disease.

Furthermore, even in cases where HIV transmission does not occur, intentionally exposing another person to the disease while aware of one's infected status can lead to second-degree felony charges for assault with a deadly weapon. Texas law broadly defines a deadly weapon as any object capable of causing death or serious injury, including infected bodily fluids such as semen. A conviction for second-degree felony assault carries a sentence of 2 to 20 years in prison.

Additionally, individuals who knowingly expose others to HIV with the intent to cause death may face charges of attempted murder, a second-degree felony. To secure an attempted murder conviction, prosecutors must demonstrate that the defendant deliberately exposed another person to the disease with the intention of infecting and causing death. In Texas, the act of exposing another person to an STD carries severe legal consequences, potentially resulting in charges of attempted murder or assault.

During Juan David Ortiz's confession, investigators confronted him about the presence of crack needles, crack pipes, condoms, and blood-contaminated needles in his truck, left behind by victims. Had Ortiz continued to carry these items in his vehicle and a child had contracted HIV or Hepatitis C as a result, he could have faced additional charges of attempted murder or assault, compounding those for which he was already convicted.

Calderon: Ortiz, I'm not going to lie to you—I'm not going to lie to you. This was in your truck. We found this in your truck: fucking crack needles, dude—crack pipes ... condoms in your truck, dude.

EJ Salinas: I would be pissed if I picked up somebody and they had that shit in my truck.

Calderon: They have blood and shit on them.

EJ Salinas: Did you get mad because someone left that in your truck?

Calderon: I don't know about you, but that's fucking *GROSS*.

EJ Salinas: You have a little girl ... grabbing one of that *SHIT*.

Calderon: Let's say you're with your family—let's say you open the truck door and throw this stuff to the side because you haven't been there in a while—innocent ... a little kid sticks himself with that ... gets hepatitis ... gets HIV.

JD: No ...

Calderon: Do you want me to show you the pictures? Do you want me to show you the pictures of what is in your truck?

JD: No ...

Calderon: You know it was in there?

JD: I don't know—using his hands to say, "I don't know?"

To individuals who engage in infidelity or have multiple sexual partners—be aware that transmitting STDs, HIV, or Hepatitis C is illegal. If you genuinely value your spouse, husband, or partner, you will refrain from jeopardizing their health by exposing them to potentially life-threatening diseases.

Numerous states have implemented legislation mandating that individuals who test positive for HIV disclose their status to both the state authorities and their current as well as past sexual or needle-sharing partners. Some jurisdictions equate HIV and AIDS to a lethal weapon through statutory provisions or judicial interpretations (Barnett, 2020).

Disclosing your HIV status to sexual or needle-sharing partners is not only ethically imperative but may also serve as a crucial defense against criminal charges (Barnett, 2020).

Under the Texas penal code, individuals with HIV or AIDS who expose others without prior notification of their positive status can face charges of assault with a deadly weapon. The law defines any object capable of causing severe harm or death as a deadly weapon, thus encompassing potential legal repercussions even in cases of consensual sexual activity (Barnett, 2020).

Moreover, intentionally exposing another person to HIV or AIDS without informing them of one's positive status with the intent to infect can lead to charges of attempted murder, regardless of consent during the sexual encounter (Barnett, 2020).

Penalties upon conviction vary depending on the specific offense. Generally, assault convictions can result in fines up to $4,000 and a maximum of one year in prison. Assault with a deadly weapon carries sentences ranging from two to twenty years in prison and fines up to $10,000. Attempted murder convictions may lead to prison terms ranging from two to ninety-nine years and fines up to $10,000. Texas law extends this criminal liability to include other sexually transmitted diseases such as syphilis or hepatitis, viewing their transmission without prior notification as bodily injury inflicted by one individual upon another.

Upon testing positive for HIV, the safest and most responsible course of action is to inform all current and previous sexual and needle-sharing partners promptly. Despite controversies, individuals with HIV are legally obliged to disclose their status and adhere to state laws to avoid criminal charges (Barnett, 2020).

Adam Plendl, who was 22 at the time, described enduring severe depression and panic attacks during the agonizing wait to ascertain whether he had contracted the virus (Young, 2012).

"It was 181 days of sheer terror, that six-month period of uncertainty," he recounted (Young, 2012).

"Individuals who are HIV positive bear both a moral and a legal obligation to disclose their status to any sexual partners. People deserve the right to choose whether to engage with an HIV-positive individual, a right that was denied to me in this instance," Plendl asserted (Young, 2012).

On September 11, 2009, Rhoades was sentenced to 25 years in prison and was subsequently transferred to the Clarinda Correctional Facility in Clarinda, Iowa, to commence serving his sentence. The enactment of criminalization laws aims to safeguard public health by preventing instances where individuals with HIV knowingly expose others to the virus without disclosing their status before engaging in sexual activities (Young, 2012).

For instance, in 2010, an HIV-positive man in Indiana was arrested for intentionally exposing over 100 women to the virus over a five-year period. Similarly, earlier this year, a man in Michigan confessed to authorities his intention to infect as many people as possible, admitting to engaging in unprotected sex with thousands of individuals over the preceding three years (Young, 2012).

Scott Burns, executive director of the National District Attorneys Association, expressed the viewpoint shared by many prosecutors regarding the need for criminal statutes in cases where individuals knowingly infect others with the HIV virus. Burns stated, "For example, if someone with HIV has unprotected sex with somebody who does not, and doesn't reveal that or doesn't disclose that and the other person becomes HIV-positive, I think that's unconscionable" (Young, 2012).

Plendl, however, disagrees with the argument that the use of a condom negates the intent to transmit, asserting, "The argument that since a condom was used there was no intent to transmit is a false statement" (Young, 2012).

Regarding the medical aspects, it is noted that while research indicates a low risk of HIV transmission through oral exposure, seminal fluid, which can contain and transmit the HIV virus, was involved prior to sexual intercourse in the case under discussion (Young, 2012).

In a recent legal case, Jimmy Billingsley, a 42-year-old man from Texas, received a 15-year prison sentence for knowingly infecting a woman with HIV through unprotected sexual intercourse, despite being aware of his HIV-positive status. Billingsley pleaded guilty to aggravated assault causing serious bodily injury and opted for a judge to determine his punishment. The woman discovered her HIV-positive status in late 2010 after a routine health examination and reported Billingsley to the authorities, stating he had pressured her repeatedly for unprotected sex (CBS DFW).

Assistant District Attorney Joshua Ross described Billingsley's actions as "egregious, dangerous, willful, and malicious" due to his deliberate non-disclosure of his HIV-positive status to multiple sexual partners (CBS DFW).

In another case, Kenneth Pinkela was convicted by a US military court for exposing a fellow soldier to HIV, a charge he denies. He served nearly a year in prison and was discharged from the US Army (Hernandez, 2013).

David Gutierrez, an HIV-positive sergeant in the US Air Force, initially sentenced to eight years for aggravated assault for failing to inform several partners of his status, had his conviction overturned on appeal in 2015, being instead found guilty of assault by battery (ProPublica).

Michael Johnson, a black gay wrestler known as Tiger Mandingo, was sentenced to 30 years in 2015 for "recklessly transmitting HIV" (Hernandez, 2013).

In Canada, Johnson Aziga was convicted of murder in 2009 for sexually transmitting HIV to two women who subsequently died of AIDS, resulting in a life sentence (ProPublica).

Samukelisiwe Mlil, a Zimbabwean woman, was convicted in 2012 of intentionally infecting her husband, although she claimed she had disclosed her HIV status to him, with no clear evidence of who infected whom (Hernandez, 2013).

In South Africa, Lovers Phiri was convicted of attempted murder for having unprotected sex with his former girlfriend without disclosing his HIV-positive status (ProPublica).

These cases highlight global prosecutions of HIV-positive individuals under specific HIV-related and general criminal laws (Hernandez, 2013).

Bioethicist Udo Schuklenk likened knowingly exposing someone to HIV without disclosure to selling a car with defective brakes, stating, "If I go out and I have a life-threatening illness and I knowingly subject you to the risk of acquiring it, I would be prosecuted" (ProPublica).

Individuals with HIV have received lengthy prison sentences for failing to disclose their status to sexual partners, even in cases where safe sex practices were observed (Hernandez, 2013).

According to ProPublica, Rhoades was sentenced to 25 years in prison by the judge for engaging in sexual activity without disclosing his HIV-positive status. His conviction, under Iowa Code Chapter 709, was for "criminal transmission of HIV," despite no actual transmission occurring to his partner, Adam Plendl, who was safeguarded by condom use and Rhoades' antiviral treatment that effectively suppressed the virus, significantly minimizing transmission risks (Hernandez, 2013).

After legal intervention, Rhoades' sentence was commuted to five years' probation, but he remains a lifetime registered aggravated sex offender, subject to severe restrictions prohibiting him from unsupervised contact with minors under 14, including family members (Hernandez, 2013).

This case is not an anomaly; over the past decade, at least 541 similar cases across 19 states have resulted in convictions or guilty pleas for failing to disclose HIV-positive status. These convictions are underpinned by laws in 35 states that criminalize HIV exposure, with 29 states categorizing it as a felony, regardless of whether transmission occurred (Hernandez, 2013).

Defendants in such cases often face lengthy prison terms, even when preventive measures like condom use are employed. Proponents of these laws argue they deter HIV spread and establish standards for disclosure in the context of an ongoing epidemic. Critics, including Linn County prosecutor Jerry Vander Sanden, equate these laws to victim-blaming, suggesting they shift responsibility from the infected person, who is aware of the danger, to the unsuspecting partner (Hernandez, 2013).

In Dallas, Larry Dunn received a 40-year prison sentence for fatally stabbing his HIV-positive lover, Cicely Bolden, after learning of her status, reflecting the severe consequences tied to these laws (Hernandez, 2013).

Since 2007, several states have expanded these laws to include Hepatitis B and C, targeting marginalized groups like intravenous drug users, who are also at high risk for HIV (Hernandez, 2013).

Nushawn Williams, convicted in 1997 for intentionally infecting multiple people with HIV, remains confined under psychiatric confinement laws despite completing his sentence, highlighting the ongoing legal repercussions for HIV-related offenses (Hernandez, 2013).

Legislative efforts, such as Senator Jesse Helms' proposed amendments, sought to criminalize healthcare workers and others with HIV, extending to prohibitions on blood and tissue donations without disclosure, underscoring the legislative response to the AIDS crisis (Hernandez, 2013).

The ALEC bill, echoed in Iowa's HIV transmission law, emphasizes the legal precedent established for prosecuting HIV exposure cases, irrespective of actual transmission (Hernandez, 2013).

While federal legislation like the Ryan White CARE Act initially addressed criminalization concerning blood and tissue donations, subsequent state-level measures have either strengthened existing laws or introduced new provisions, particularly enhancing penalties when law enforcement personnel are affected (Hernandez, 2013).

For instance, Nebraska's 2011 law escalated penalties for HIV-positive individuals who spit or bite public safety officers, illustrating the varied and stringent applications of these statutes (Hernandez, 2013).

Three states — Mississippi, Nebraska, and Tennessee — have criminalized exposing someone to Hepatitis B or C. In Nebraska and Tennessee, this offense constitutes a misdemeanor, contrasting sharply with HIV exposure, which is classified as a felony, despite Hepatitis B being potentially 100 times more infectious than HIV, as reported by ProPublica (Hernandez, 2013).

On June 26, 2008, Nick Rhoades was at his residence in Plainfield, Iowa, when he received a chat invitation on Gay.com, a dating and social networking platform. The sender, Adam Plendl, a 22-year-old student at the University of Northern Iowa, initiated contact (Hernandez, 2013).

At 3:00 a.m. that morning, Rhoades and Plendl engaged in conversation. Plendl invited Rhoades to his new apartment in Cedar Falls, situated approximately 30 miles south of Plainfield, where they spent hours drinking pomegranate vodka martinis, smoking marijuana, unpacking Plendl's belongings, and bonding over shared experiences with bipolar disorder. Subsequently, they engaged in sexual activity (Hernandez, 2013).

According to ProPublica, a few nights later, Plendl, while sharing a late-night cigarette with Jordan Brown, learned through informal channels that Rhoades was reportedly "ill." Alarmed by the potential exposure to HIV, Plendl rushed to the emergency room at Sartori Memorial Hospital nearby (Hernandez, 2013).

Plendl's intent was to obtain a short-term emergency regimen of HIV medications, effective if administered within 72 hours of exposure, to prevent infection. Frustrated by the hospital's lack of clarity on the procedure, Plendl sought assistance at Covenant Medical Center's emergency room in Waterloo, where a registered nurse, Brandy Weida-Cooper, admitted him. Hospital records indicate that Weida-Cooper alerted the police, although Plendl claims he did not initiate police involvement (Hernandez, 2013).

By 4:02 a.m., a Cedar Falls patrol officer was present in the emergency room, ready to record Plendl's statement. Notably, nearly a quarter of convictions and guilty pleas in similar cases involved women, including purported sex workers (Hernandez, 2013).

In St. Louis, Nigaila Gibbs, aged 20, was arrested during an undercover operation in 2010. Born with HIV, Gibbs turned to prostitution after leaving Missouri's foster care system. Law enforcement accused her of engaging in sexual activity with numerous clients without disclosing her HIV status, although Gibbs maintained she consistently practiced safe sex. Following her arrest, St. Louis County police encouraged potential victims to come forward, though no infections or charges for soliciting a prostitute were reported (Hernandez, 2013).

Gibbs pleaded guilty to engaging in prostitution while knowingly HIV-positive and received a five-year prison sentence in Missouri. Presently, web search results for Gibbs's name yield blog posts and forum discussions with titles like "AIDS Whore Nigaila Gibbs May Have Infected Hundreds!" and "Fat ugly prostitute infects over 100 clients w/ HIV" (Hernandez, 2013).

Thomas Tompkins was in the final month of his sentence at Ohio's Richland Correctional Institution when a guard caught him engaging in oral sex with another inmate in the prison library. State authorities investigated whether the encounter was consensual; both inmates confirmed it was. However, Tompkins faced felony charges of assault with HIV after admitting he had not disclosed his HIV-positive status to the other inmate (Hernandez, 2013).

JANUARY 20, 2024

Author: Do you have HIV or STDs?

JD: No ... I don't have any diseases. It was stated during my trial— when asked if I had HIV or STDs—that I don't have HIV or any diseases. I was tested for all that ... twice. I know there was hearsay about that. It's not true.

"JOHNS" AND THE NEW LAW

"Juan embodied the literal essence of being a 'John.' He even bears the name 'John.' No pun intended."

"Prostitution stings are increasingly prevalent due to the elevation of solicitation to a felony offense. An agreement to exchange something of value for sexual activity suffices for prosecution, irrespective of whether a meeting or actual transaction occurs.

According to Texas law, prostitution entails agreeing to receive compensation for engaging in sexual conduct. Initially categorized as a Class B misdemeanor, punishable by up to 180 days in jail and a $2,000 fine, repeat offenders face a Class A misdemeanor, penalizable by up to one year in jail and a $4,000 fine.

Perpetrators of solicitation—commonly referred to as 'Johns'—now confront more severe, felony charges compared to prostitutes. Effective September 1, 2021, solicitation of prostitution graduated to felony status under extensive legislation targeting human trafficking.

Charges for solicitation vary, ranging from a state jail felony to a second-degree felony based on individual circumstances:

- First-time offenders may receive a state jail felony, with sentences spanning six months to two years and a fine up to $10,000.

- Previous offenders face a third-degree felony, involving imprisonment for 2 to 10 years and a maximum $10,000 fine.

Merely discussing monetary exchange for sex can lead to legal repercussions, regardless of intent or whether the offer was casual or unfulfilled."

ARRESTS

During Juan David Ortiz's December 2022 trial, Erika Peña testified against him. His defense attorney, Joel Perez, highlighted her occupation, substance use disorder, and prior charges of assaulting a law enforcement officer and resisting arrest (*Laredo Morning Times*, 2022).

According to the *Laredo Morning Times*, Erika Peña was arrested in May 2019 following a domestic disturbance at her residence, where she allegedly threatened a family member's life. During her apprehension, Peña resisted arrest, attempting to evade capture by kicking an officer. Despite her resistance, law enforcement successfully subdued her and transported her to Webb County Jail. At the time of her mugshot on May 7, 2019, Peña appeared under the influence, displaying a slender physique and blonde hair.

Further reports from the *Laredo Morning Times* indicate Peña's additional arrest for assaulting a Laredo police officer, culminating in charges of assault on a peace officer, categorized as a second-degree felony. Responding to a distress call on March 14 in the 2900 block of San Bernardo Avenue, officers encountered a man with visible injuries to his face and chest, alleging Peña as the assailant. Police entered the residence, where Peña complied with directives to descend from the second floor. Following her arrest, Peña's confrontational behavior persisted, leading to her striking an officer and exhibiting agitation during the booking process.

Subsequent events documented by the *Laredo Morning Times* detail Peña's recurring encounters with law enforcement, including an arrest for child abandonment due to negligence, classified as a state jail felony. Her involvement in an overdose incident on Guerrero Street underscored her struggles with substance abuse, necessitating medical intervention at Laredo Medical Center. Peña's lapse in methadone treatment, intended to manage her heroin addiction, contributed to her deteriorating condition, prompting intervention by Child Protective Services.

During her hospitalization, Peña admitted to using "China white," a potent form of heroin laced with fentanyl, attributing her compromised state to withdrawal symptoms. Her admission to Laredo Medical Center due to respiratory distress and unconsciousness necessitated intensive monitoring, highlighting ongoing challenges linked to illicit substance use.

Erika Isamar Peña faces charges for two Class A misdemeanors: Assault Causes Bodily Injury - Family Member, under Texas Penal Code §22.01(a)(1), and Resist Arrest, Search, or Transport, under Texas Penal Code §38.03(a). The offenses occurred on March 14, 2023. The case, involving all misdemeanors, was filed on June 13, 2024, in County Court at Law #2. A court notice was mailed on June 18, 2024, for a scheduled hearing on September 30, 2024, at 9:00 a.m. However, the notice was returned on June 24, 2024, due to an insufficient address.

WHAT WENT WRONG WITH THIS CASE?

Juan David Ortiz is currently appealing his case. Ortiz should have pleaded "Not Guilty" due to temporary insanity from the outset as part of his defense strategy. Although challenging to prove, he could have utilized the Insanity Defense in his appeal, bolstered by testimony from his PTSD specialist, who diagnosed him while he was under the influence of eight medications and alcohol.

Ortiz's legal representation was ineffective. Once the death penalty was off the table, his attorney Joel Perez appeared to relax, knowing the likely outcome would be life without parole. This attitude was evident in court, where crucial witnesses such as Ortiz's PTSD doctors, former employers, and friends were not called to testify, leaving the defense without a coherent strategy. Observers noted that Ortiz's defense was severely lacking.

In his closing statement, Perez urged the jury to find Ortiz guilty of murder but not to categorize him as a serial killer, a move that could be perceived as detrimental to Ortiz's defense. This action raises concerns about the effectiveness of Perez's counsel and could serve as grounds for an appeal. The public criticism on social media further underscored the perceived inadequacy of Ortiz's defense team.

There is also an argument that Ortiz's Miranda rights were violated during his interrogation, as he explicitly refused to speak with law enforcement and declined to sign a waiver of his rights before ultimately confessing after being detained for over ten hours and offered a meal as an incentive.

Moreover, the defense failed to request a gag order despite extensive media coverage, potentially biasing the jury. The composition of the predominantly female jury (with only four men out of twelve) in a case involving female victims further complicates the fairness of the trial. The jury's inability to witness Ortiz's emotional reactions regarding his children also detracted from presenting his human side.

Ortiz's family was misled by the defense team into believing there was a viable chance of acquittal based on the Miranda rights issue, adding to the list of grievances constituting ineffective counsel. His appeal hinges largely on these missteps and procedural errors that marred his trial.

JANUARY 15, 2024

Ortiz claimed that his Miranda rights were violated when he requested legal counsel three times but was denied. Authorities allegedly tampered with his truck, removing his firearm from the glove compartment, inserting a magazine into the unloaded gun, and placing it in the driver's door panel, subsequently using it as evidence against him. This situation invokes the fruit of the poisonous tree doctrine. Allegedly, promises were made, negotiating a plea for first-degree murder. Video interrogation statements and transcripts where Ortiz requested an attorney and discussed plea deals were purportedly excluded.

The jury did not receive a complete view of Ortiz's version of events. Ortiz contends that he had ineffective legal representation. If Ortiz's claims hold true, this case may potentially reach the Supreme Court and be dismissed on procedural grounds concerning Ortiz's treatment. Such oversights can prove costly in legal proceedings and may ultimately backfire. Ortiz should have been provided legal representation upon his initial request. Authorities could have continued their investigation after Ortiz obtained legal counsel.

Belief in the Constitution and the principles of due process underscores the importance of upholding rights. Advocates may argue that the end justifies the means, asserting that any action was justified to apprehend Ortiz, regardless of the consequences. However, such arguments undermine fundamental rights. This is not characteristic of a democratic society, such as the United States, distinguishing it from authoritarian states like China or Russia. Upholding the law necessitates reasoned adherence, free from emotional or public pressures. Even Ortiz, as an accused individual, maintains rights because of the protections guaranteed by the U.S. Constitution, distinguishing the country from less democratic regimes.

LANDMARK CASE

Moments prior to the commencement of a homicide trial yesterday, D.C. Superior Court Judge Henry H. Kennedy Jr. intervened in the proceedings and invalidated a recorded statement made by the defendant, citing a Supreme Court decision issued less than 24 hours earlier. As a result, jurors were dismissed, and federal prosecutors are now deliberating over the potential appeal of Judge Kennedy's ruling in the case involving 19-year-old Lowell Green, accused in the 1988 fatal shooting of a District resident. Kennedy's decisive action underscored the significant ramifications of the Supreme Court's recent ruling in *Minnick v. Mississippi*, which explicitly prohibits law enforcement officers from interrogating suspects outside the presence of their legal counsel subsequent to the suspect's request for legal representation (Torry, 1990).

The 6 to 2 decision represents an extension of the landmark 1966 *Miranda* ruling, mandating that criminal suspects be informed of their rights to remain silent and consult with an attorney. The ruling emphasizes that even following a suspect's consultation with an attorney, police are prohibited from attempting further questioning unless the attorney is present. Defense attorneys have welcomed the Supreme Court's decision, noting its probable impact on high-profile cases involving extensive investigative efforts by law enforcement (Torry, 1990).

"The ruling's primary impact will be felt in cases where law enforcement, driven by their resolve to resolve a case, seek multiple opportunities to persuade a defendant to waive their right to counsel and engage in dialogue," remarked defense lawyer G. Allen Dale. "The *Minnick* decision establishes a clear legal standard, eliminating discretion for law enforcement and lower courts. Once a suspect requests an attorney, questioning *must* cease" (Torry, 1990).

Last week, Kennedy denied a defense motion to suppress the aforementioned statement. However, following his review of the *Minnick* decision, he reversed his stance and excluded the statement from evidence. The U.S. Attorney highlighted that a critical aspect of the Supreme Court's ruling pertains to its broader application by judges in cases such as Green's, where a defendant secures legal representation in one matter but is questioned in an unrelated case (Torry, 1990).

The Court's establishment of the *Edwards* presumption dictates that upon a suspect invoking their right to counsel, any subsequent waiver of Miranda rights is deemed involuntary unless counsel is present or the suspect initiates further communication ("*Edwards v. Arizona*," 2023).

JANUARY 16, 2024

JD: I was very—good at my job. I was in DISRUPT detail. Our job was to disrupt. I know the difference between what a "bail out" means due to my job and the case I helped try in court. I didn't "bail out" from my truck on the night of my arrest. One of my cases made it to the United States Court of Appeals. Look for *United States of America, Plaintiff–Appellee v. Jesse Dominguez*, Case Number: 804 F.3d 702 (5th Cir. 2015) in *LexisNexis*.

It happened on December 17, 2013, and was decided on October 21, 2015. This case was prosecuted by Assistant United States Attorney Sarah Wannarka. I come out in that case. The judge was U.S. District Judge Fred Biery. I was a U.S. Border Patrol Agent (USBP Agent) at that time. Their court records have my title as U.S. Customs and Border Protection Agent. They got my title wrong. I don't know why they keep getting my title wrong ... most of the time.

Accordingly, the judgment of the district court is reversed and vacated, and the case is remanded for entry of a judgment of acquittal (*United States v. Dominguez*, 611 Fed.Appx. 247, 247 (5th Cir.2015) (per curiam)).

The district court rendered the following comprehensive findings:

U.S. Customs and Border Protection Agent Juan David Ortiz testified during the *Motion to Suppress* hearing on February 27, 2014. Agent Ortiz served in the United States Navy from 2001 to 2009 and earned a Bachelor's Degree from American Military University during his service. Joining the U.S. Customs and Border Protection in 2009, Agent Ortiz received specialized training in narcotics and human trafficking investigations. His qualifications include a Master's Degree from St. Mary's University. Agent Ortiz's expertise includes extensive observation of traffic patterns on Interstate (IH) 35 and substantial experience in trafficking investigations, rendering his testimony credible.

On December 17, 2013, Agent Ortiz conducted roving patrol in a marked unit on IH 35 near mile marker 112, close to Moore, Texas, within the Western District of Texas. Mile marker 112 lies approximately 112 miles north of the Texas/Mexico border.

Agent Ortiz was part of a Highway Interdiction team tasked with monitoring IH–35 traffic to intercept vehicles involved in narcotics and human trafficking. He became familiar with typical traffic on this stretch of highway, such as oil field trucks, hunting and ranch vehicles, and tourist vehicles.

Around 10:30 a.m. on December 17, 2013, Agent Ortiz observed a maroon Ford Expedition traveling southbound on IH–35 occupied by Crystal Doerr and Jesse Dominguez. Agent Ortiz noted the vehicle's uniqueness compared to typical traffic—it was not a work vehicle, lacked mud or ranch-related dirt, and did not appear to carry luggage suggesting a trip. No traffic stop was conducted at this time.

At approximately 1:30 p.m. that same day, Agent Ortiz observed the same maroon Ford Expedition traveling northbound on IH–35, now with an additional passenger in the back seat whom he had not seen earlier.

Dispatch informed Agent Ortiz that the vehicle had not passed through any border checkpoints between its southbound and northbound journeys, suggesting possible use of alternate routes to evade checkpoints.

Agent Ortiz trailed the vehicle for 2–3 miles, yet neither Dominguez nor Doerr acknowledged his presence. He noted their stiffness and forward-facing demeanor as unusual.

Upon closer observation, Agent Ortiz identified a small child in the back seat, not secured in a visible child safety seat.

Agent Ortiz ran the vehicle's plates, which traced back to Crystal Doerr of San Antonio, Texas. He observed Dominguez driving erratically—traveling at 15 mph in a 75-mph zone, weaving on the shoulder, and intermittently tapping the brakes.

The presence of an unrestrained child in a vehicle exhibiting erratic behavior on the interstate raised suspicion of potential trafficking.

Agent Ortiz conducted a traffic stop near mile marker 120 on IH 35.

Based on the above observations, reasonable suspicion existed to conduct an investigative traffic stop to further investigate whether Dominguez and Doerr were involved in child trafficking.

At the scene, Agent Ortiz discovered that the 4-year-old girl from Mexico was illegally present in the United States. Dominguez and Doerr confessed, waiving their Miranda rights at the U.S. Customs and Border Protection station. They admitted to picking up the child in Dilley, Texas, from smugglers who transported her across the Texas/Mexico border. Dominguez and Doerr intended to transport the child to San Antonio for financial compensation, leading to their arrest for violating Title 8, United States Code, Section 1324, Bringing in and Harboring Certain Aliens (*United States v. Dominguez*, 2015).

In its brief, the government cited *United States v. Munoz–Martinez*, 435 Fed. Appx. 333 (5th Cir.2011) (per curiam), as a comparable case multiple times. Notably, neither defendant addressed this case in their response (*United States v. Dominguez*, 2015).

The Munoz–Martinez panel expounded upon the events as follows: On the evening of December 2, 2009, Fernando Munoz–Martinez was driving a pickup truck south on Interstate 35. Near Artesia Wells, Texas, approximately 56 miles north of the Mexican border, two Border Patrol agents observed a pickup truck exiting onto Highway 133. Ten to 15 minutes later, the agents witnessed what appeared to be the same truck returning onto I-35, heading north. After trailing the vehicle for seven miles, the agents suspected it was engaged in alien smuggling. They conducted an investigatory stop and discovered eight illegal aliens in the truck, including the driver, Munoz–Martinez (*United States v. Dominguez*, 2015).

The agents testified that a license plate check revealed Munoz–Martinez had not recently passed through the border checkpoint on I-35 (*United States v. Dominguez*, 2015).

Additionally, the agents testified that the area where Munoz–Martinez was apprehended is notorious for drug and alien-smuggling activities. Moreover, Munoz–Martinez's purple, low-riding pickup truck raised suspicion, as it was not typical of the traffic in the area, which predominantly consisted of vehicles related to the oil industry, ranching, and hunting. Testimony indicated that such a vehicle traveling on the state highway in this area after exiting the interstate was unusual (*United States v. Dominguez*, 2015).

Munoz–Martinez's driving behavior also aroused suspicion. Initially traveling south on I-35, he exited into a rural area devoid of residences, then returned northbound on I-35. While agents drove parallel to Munoz–Martinez's vehicle, they observed the head of a previously unseen third passenger briefly emerge between the driver and the second passenger, before retracting. Furthermore, it was noted that Munoz–Martinez significantly reduced his vehicle's speed by half, to approximately 30 miles per hour in a 65 miles-per-hour zone, upon becoming aware of the agents' presence, despite not exceeding the speed limit (*United States v. Dominguez*, 2015).

Moreover, it is relevant that neither agent had served with the Border Patrol for more than a year and a half. One agent provided testimony based on his encounters with smugglers and stated his involvement in several smuggling apprehensions after witnessing "bailouts" on five or six occasions. Such testimony indicates that despite his brief tenure, he had accrued pertinent experience and possessed substantial knowledge (*United States v. Dominguez*, 2015).

The factual parallels between Munoz–Martinez and Dominguez are extensive: both apprehensions occurred on Interstate 35 between Laredo and San Antonio, a known corridor for drug and alien smuggling. In both instances, Border Patrol agents initially observed the vehicles traveling southbound, later encountering them again northbound on the same highway. There was no evidence that either vehicle had recently passed through a border checkpoint. Initially seen with only two occupants in the front seat while southbound, both vehicles were later observed northbound with a visible third passenger (in Dominguez, a four-year-old girl). In both cases, attempts were made to conceal the newly added passenger. Both vehicles were atypical for the area's typical traffic. Agents followed both vehicles northbound for several miles to establish reasonable suspicion before initiating a stop. Upon sighting the Border Patrol truck, both drivers noticeably slowed their speed. Furthermore, both drivers exhibited multiple behaviors deemed suspicious by officers based on their experience and training. In both cases, the agents possessed significant experience and expertise in alien-smuggling interdiction (*United States v. Dominguez*, 2015).

Despite these notable similarities, the Munoz–Martinez panel upheld the denial of the motion to suppress and affirmed the conviction, while the Dominguez panel, with limited explanation, found a Fourth Amendment violation and directed an acquittal. Consequently, Munoz–Martinez, the admitted human smuggler, continued to serve his sentence, whereas the confessed child smugglers in Dominguez were acquitted (*United States v. Dominguez*, 2015).

JD: I assisted in prosecuting a case. It was reversed using *United States v. Brignoni-Ponce*, 422 U.S. 873 (1975)—a landmark case in which the Supreme Court determined it was a violation of the Fourth Amendment for a roving patrol car to stop a vehicle solely based on the driver's Mexican descent. The Court ruled that a roving patrol car must possess articulable facts that provide an officer with reasonable suspicion that the person is transporting illegal aliens beyond their ethnicity. The Court handed down a unanimous 9–0 decision affirming the Circuit Court's ruling ("*United States v. Brignoni-Ponce*," 2023).

JD: I also used *United States v. Martinez-Fuerte*, 428 U.S. 543 (1976) as another landmark case.

In *United States v. Martinez-Fuerte* (1976), the defendant, Amado Martinez-Fuerte, was apprehended for transporting two undocumented Mexican aliens who had entered the United States via the Port of San Ysidro in San Diego, California. Upon traveling northward, their vehicle was intercepted at a permanent checkpoint located on Interstate 5 between Oceanside and San Clemente, where the passengers admitted their unlawful status. Martinez-Fuerte was subsequently charged with two counts of unlawfully transporting aliens. He sought to suppress the evidence, arguing that the checkpoint stop constituted a Fourth Amendment violation. However, the court denied his motion, leading to his conviction on both counts ("*United States v. Martinez-Fuerte*," 2023).

United States v. Martinez-Fuerte (1976) was a pivotal ruling by the United States Supreme Court permitting the establishment of permanent checkpoints by the United States Border Patrol along public highways leading to and from the Mexican border. The Court determined that such checkpoints do not contravene the Fourth Amendment ("*United States v. Martinez-Fuerte*," 2023).

PAXIL SUICIDE AND HOMICIDE LAWSUITS

Paxil, known generically as paroxetine hydrochloride, belongs to the class of SSRIs commonly prescribed for depression and anxiety disorders. However, both the brand-name and generic versions of Paxil carry a serious risk: individuals may be more prone to committing suicide or homicide while under its influence. Attorneys at Baum Hedlund are currently investigating cases involving Paxil-related suicides, representing families whose loved ones have taken their lives while on Paxil, as well as individuals who have attempted suicide during Paxil treatment (Baum Hedlund, n.d.).

Baum Hedlund has a distinguished record in litigation, securing over $4 billion for their clients over four decades, with some of the largest settlements and verdicts in antidepressant litigation history. This underscores their capacity to advocate effectively for victims and catalyze changes within the pharmaceutical industry (Baum Hedlund, n.d.).

A notable case is that of Wendy Dolin, whose husband, Stewart Dolin, tragically committed suicide only six days after beginning treatment with a generic form of Paxil. In 2017, an Illinois jury awarded Wendy Dolin $3 million in damages, marking a significant legal stance against GlaxoSmithKline (GSK), the original manufacturer of Paxil. This verdict emphasized the responsibility of generic drug manufacturers to provide adequate warnings to consumers regarding potential side effects (Baum Hedlund, n.d.).

During the Dolin trial, pivotal evidence emerged from GlaxoSmithKline itself. Dr. David Ross, a former FDA official, testified regarding GSK's 1991 submission to the FDA, which allegedly misrepresented suicide data from Paxil clinical trials. This included reporting a higher number of suicides in the placebo group compared to the actual trial data, thereby downplaying the suicide risks associated with paroxetine (Baum Hedlund, n.d.).

The trial also revealed other critical findings:

Evidence of publication bias: In 1995, psychiatrists affiliated with GSK published findings suggesting that paroxetine reduced suicide rates, influencing medical perceptions despite internal data indicating otherwise.

Confirmation of increased suicide risk: GSK's internal analysis in 2006 affirmed that patients taking Paxil faced a nearly sevenfold increase in suicide attempts compared to those on placebo.

FDA scrutiny: A 2006 FDA analysis highlighted a 2.7-fold increased risk of suicidal behavior with Paxil across clinical trials involving adults, a finding deemed statistically significant by the FDA's Director of Neurological Products (Baum Hedlund, n.d.).

By the end of 2006, substantial evidence had accumulated suggesting that Paxil posed serious risks across age groups, contradicting earlier assertions by GSK. Michael Baum, senior managing shareholder of Baum Hedlund, criticized GSK for allegedly concealing and downplaying these risks throughout two decades of litigation (Baum Hedlund, n.d.).

Despite the presence of a "black box" warning on Paxil labels regarding suicidal ideation and behavior among children, adolescents, and young adults up to 24 years old, failures to extend these warnings to older adults may have contributed to further tragedies (Baum Hedlund, n.d.).

Given Paxil's widespread prescription for various mental health conditions, questions arise regarding attributing suicidal behaviors solely to drug defects rather than underlying mental illnesses. Victims of defective antidepressants, witnessing their loved ones' suicides, may question this attribution (Baum Hedlund, n.d.).

In the Dolin trial, jurors deliberated over conflicting viewpoints from psychiatric and pharmacological experts for five weeks. Ultimately, they concluded that existing research and medical understanding supported the notion that Paxil, including its generic form paroxetine, could induce suicidal behaviors in individuals over 24 years old (Baum Hedlund, n.d.).

Another troubling side effect linked to Paxil is emotional blunting, characterized by apathy or emotional indifference—a recognized phenomenon in SSRIs like Paxil. Psychiatrist Dr. David Healy highlighted during the Dolin trial that emotional blunting, coupled with akathisia, could diminish an individual's awareness of the consequences of self-harm or harm to others, potentially precipitating suicidal or homicidal thoughts (Baum Hedlund, n.d.).

According to Dr. Healy's testimony in the Dolin trial, upon the introduction of SSRIs into the market, researchers early on observed that individuals who self-harmed while using these medications tended to do so in markedly violent manners. In our comprehensive investigation as prominent legal representatives, we identified 22 cases of suicide during the Paxil clinical trials, with 16 of these suicides exhibiting violent characteristics, including instances involving firearms (Paxil suicide lawsuits, n.d.).

Healy noted, "One of the things that struck people fairly early on with the effects of these pills was that the nature, the way people harmed themselves, often seemed to be disproportionately violent" (Paxil suicide lawsuits, n.d.).

GlaxoSmithKline (GSK), originally responsible for Paxil, transferred full responsibility for the drug to Apotex in January 2014. Despite not creating the drug, Apotex now manufactures both Paxil and its generic paroxetine, assuming responsibility for their labeling and promotional campaigns.

Similar to the accountability enforced upon GSK for inadequate warnings about Paxil's hazardous side effects, Apotex, as the current manufacturer, must also face legal scrutiny. As Canada's largest pharmaceutical company and a major global generics manufacturer, Apotex produces over 300 pharmaceuticals, including Paxil. Unfortunately, the current Paxil/paroxetine label continues to neglect to caution adults over 24 about the heightened suicide risk—an omission Baum Hedlund highlighted in a letter to Apotex on September 1, 2017 (Paxil suicide lawsuits, n.d.).

The existing Paxil/paroxetine label remains scientifically, ethically, and legally indefensible by failing to alert healthcare providers and consumers about the risk of suicide in adults over 24 (Paxil suicide lawsuits, n.d.).

This oversight dangerously misguides doctors and patients in two critical ways:

- It implies that the risk of suicide does not extend beyond the age of 24.

- It suggests that known Paxil side effects are merely symptoms of a purported illness, placing both patients and doctors in precarious positions (Paxil suicide lawsuits, n.d.).

To challenge this unethical labeling, Baum Hedlund's attorneys formally requested Apotex in 2017 to promptly rectify the deficiencies in the Paxil label, ensuring it properly warns of the elevated risk of adult suicidal behavior linked to Paxil and paroxetine. Failure to comply would indicate Apotex's prioritization of financial gain over public safety (Paxil suicide lawsuits, n.d.).

Both GSK and Apotex have long been aware of Paxil's suicide risks. While the current label now addresses risks in children and young adults, it neglects to do so for older adults (Paxil suicide lawsuits, n.d.).

The Dolin v. Smithkline Beecham Corp. trial commenced in March 2017 in Chicago, Illinois. Plaintiff Wendy Dolin brought the lawsuit against GSK in 2012, alleging that her husband, Stewart Dolin, a partner at Reed Smith, died by suicide induced by paroxetine (Paxil suicide lawsuits, n.d.).

Leading attorneys Michael Baum and Brent Wisner, renowned for their extensive experience in antidepressant defect litigation, including cases involving antidepressant birth defects, medication-induced violence, and generic Paxil suicide claims, represented Wendy Dolin in securing $3 million from GSK to compensate for her family's suffering and losses (Paxil suicide lawsuits, n.d.).

Stewart Dolin initiated paroxetine treatment in July 2010. GSK, the developer and marketer of Paxil, was responsible for the drug's research, development, and the accuracy of its labeling (Paxil suicide lawsuits, n.d.).

On July 15, 2010, shortly after a business lunch, Stewart Dolin, visibly agitated, walked to a Chicago Transit Authority station and, observed by a witness, leapt in front of an oncoming train, resulting in his death (Paxil suicide lawsuits, n.d.).

The Paxil warning label, mandated to be copied by generic manufacturers, falsely asserts that the risk of suicidality does not extend beyond age 24, despite GSK's clinical trials indicating a nearly 700% increase in the risk of suicidality with Paxil use. Judge James B. Zagel of the Northern District of Illinois, Eastern Division, ruled in favor of allowing Ms. Dolin's action against GSK for negligence, product liability, and fraud, despite GSK not manufacturing the specific generic version that led to Mr. Dolin's death. The lawsuit was filed on July 9, 2012 (Paxil suicide lawsuits, n.d.).

In her original 2012 complaint, the plaintiff accused GSK of negligently and fraudulently misrepresenting paroxetine's safety and efficacy, manipulating clinical trial data to obscure the drug's suicidal behavior risk, and falsely promoting its safety and efficacy through ghostwritten articles and salesforce visits to physicians (Paxil suicide lawsuits, n.d.).

In 2014, a federal judge in Chicago largely denied GSK's motion for summary judgment in Wendy Dolin's wrongful death lawsuit, affirming that GSK was negligent in paroxetine's design and drug labeling (Paxil suicide lawsuits, n.d.).

In his ruling, Judge Zagel asserted that GSK's negligence regarding paroxetine's design and warning label could foreseeably lead to harm for consumers using subsequent generic versions of the drug (Paxil suicide lawsuits, n.d.).

Judge Zagel emphasized that GSK's non-involvement in manufacturing the specific generic drug consumed by Mr. Dolin did not diminish the potential impact of GSK's alleged tortious actions on the plaintiff's injury. He reiterated that the negligence attributed to GSK extends beyond the Paxil manufacturing process and could potentially cause harm to users of all paroxetine formulations, including generics (Paxil suicide lawsuits, n.d.).

The judge also dismissed several arguments from GSK as lacking merit, which appeared to obfuscate rather than clarify the issues at hand.

Instances of suicides linked to Paxil usage further underscore the serious implications raised in litigation. These include a 58-year-old woman who hanged herself after eight days on Paxil, a 42-year-old who overdosed on another substance after ten days, a 56-year-old who drowned herself after seven weeks, a 50-year-old man who hanged himself in the third month, and another 58-year-old woman who hanged herself in the fifth month of Paxil use. Additionally, an 18-year-old woman committed suicide six days after discontinuing Paxil following a clinical trial ("Paxil suicide lawsuits," n.d.).

By 1989, GSK was aware of five suicides during Paxil clinical trials and reported 40 suicide attempts among patients actively using the drug, indicating prior knowledge of its potential risks ("Paxil suicide lawsuits," n.d.).

The pharmaceutical industry's unethical practices, including ghostwriting of clinical trial reports, have perpetuated misleading conclusions about Paxil's safety profile despite widespread evidence of data manipulation and subsequent patient harm ("Paxil suicide lawsuits," n.d.).

Notably, both Paxil and its generic counterparts can induce akathisia, a medication-induced condition characterized by severe internal restlessness and mental disturbance, which has been consistently associated with increased risks of suicidal and homicidal behaviors ("Paxil suicide lawsuits," n.d.).

FEBRUARY 10, 2024

Author: You were right. Hector Humberto Rodriguez made headlines in the *Laredo Morning Times* when allegations surfaced that he had sexually assaulted two female inmates while employed as a former Webb County jailer at the Webb County Jail. This information, conveyed in April 2023, has proven prophetic. Rodriguez was apprehended on February 17, 2022, facing state charges. According to the federal indictment, he stands accused of violating the civil rights of these women through coercive sexual assaults during their incarceration. Each of the five charges in the indictment carries the potential penalty of life imprisonment and fines amounting to $250,000. The FBI and the Department of Justice's Office of Inspector General conducted the investigation.

JD: I told you. I have no reason to lie to you. Every detail I'm telling you is true. I was there when this occurred. Jose Hernandez was the commander and jail administrator at that time. Hector did what he did under the leadership of Jose Hernandez and Sheriff Martin Cuellar. Jose Hernandez is now the Chief of Police at Laredo College. The Sheriff would say that I was the *vigilante* at the jail, since I was making complaints about the jail for violating inmates' rights and treating us in an inhumane way.

Recent incidents of mass violence, such as Joseph Wesbecker's shooting of his co-workers in Virginia, the Virginia Tech murders, the Columbine shootings, and the Fort Hood shootings, underscore concerns about the dangers posed by antidepressant and SSRI medications to public safety. These medications have been linked to homicidal ideation, leading to acts of public violence and suicides. The pharmaceutical industry seeks to capitalize on returning veterans as a substantial customer base for psychiatric drugs. Given their training and access to firearms, veterans grappling with Post Traumatic Stress Disorder (PTSD) present significant mental health challenges that the government, through Medicaid/Medicare, may soon shoulder the financial burden for pharmaceutical companies ("Mass murder and psychiatric drugs," n.d.).

These large pharmaceutical entities exert considerable influence, notably within the President's New Freedom Commission on Mental Health, advocating for widespread marketing of SSRIs and other psychotropic drugs to veterans with PTSD. Another targeted demographic is the expanding prison population, particularly those preparing for release and becoming eligible for Medicaid/Medicare coverage.

Upon their introduction in the late 1980s and early 1990s, SSRIs like Prozac, Paxil, and Zoloft were initially praised, but reports soon emerged of increased violent behaviors, including suicides and homicides. Concerns escalated in 2003 when British authorities and the U.S. Food and Drug Administration highlighted unpublished studies revealing heightened suicide risks among children and teenagers taking Paxil. Despite evidence of suicidal and homicidal behaviors in adults on SSRIs, pharmaceutical companies and mainstream medical professionals often downplay these risks by attributing them to the underlying depression ("Mass murder and psychiatric drugs," n.d.).

While SSRIs are not universally effective or indicated for every case of depression, they can exacerbate conditions. These drugs may induce severe side effects that impair judgment and impulse control, particularly when administered in excessive doses, leading to cognitive disturbances and other brain dysfunctions. In combat veterans suffering from PTSD, impulsive behavior coupled with cognitive impairment poses significant dangers.

Furthermore, SSRIs can precipitate manic-like symptoms in individuals with bipolar disorder, a condition frequently overlooked during prescription. Despite pharmaceutical claims that these drugs reduce suicide and homicide risks, questions persist regarding their actual impact on public safety.

The tragic Fort Hood shooting on November 5, 2009, where a military psychiatrist killed 13 people and wounded 30 others, serves as a stark reminder of the risks associated with psychiatric drug treatments among military personnel and veterans. Similar incidents, such as the Northern Illinois University mass shooting by Stephen Kazmierczak, who had been taking Paxil, underscore the need for vigilant monitoring and reconsideration of psychiatric drug therapies.

In many legal cases involving pharmaceutical companies, court records are sealed and evidence of misconduct concealed from public scrutiny. Settlements frequently include gag orders and exemptions from discovery, shielding the public from awareness even when numerous deaths and injuries result. Pharmaceutical companies allocate substantial resources to legal defense strategies, including countersuits and intimidation tactics against witnesses, particularly medical professionals acting as expert witnesses.

The systemic failure of our courts and regulatory bodies to protect the public from the risks posed by psychiatric drugs raises urgent concerns. When will public officials acknowledge the genuine dangers posed by psychotropic medications, which disrupt brain activity and can incite violent thoughts?

See the following list of traumatic incidents and deaths associated with antidepressant use:

In 2004, on July 26, Mary Ellen Moffitt, 37, was killed by the antidepressant Paxil/Seroxat (paroxetine).

William J. Heck, 35, fell victim to violence linked to Paxil/Seroxat (paroxetine) on February 22, 2004.

Denise Martin, 53, experienced distressing dreams of killing associated with Paxil/Seroxat in December 2003.

In June 2003, "Mum", aged 32, engaged in attempted murder/suicide under the influence of Paxil/Seroxat and Effexor.

George Harold Davis, 46, was killed due to withdrawal rage from Paxil/Seroxat in June 2003.

Carol Ackels, 40, tragically killed her daughter under the influence of Paxil/Seroxat (paroxetine) on July 24, 2002.

Lee Sims, 68, was killed on July 12, 2002, while taking antidepressants, specifically Paxil/Seroxat (paroxetine).

Cindy Gail Countess, 49, was killed by Paxil/Seroxat (paroxetine) on May 3, 2002.

Michael McDermott, 42, committed killings associated with Prozac, Paxil, and Desyrel (trazodone) on December 26, 2000.

Donald Schell, 60, tragically died from consuming two tablets of Paxil/Seroxat (paroxetine) on February 13, 1998.

In Teens:

Dustin Lynch, 16, was killed at home linked to Paxil/Seroxat on November 2, 2002.

School violence claimed Sean McEvoy, 15, on April 10, 2002, associated with Paxil/Seroxat.

Christopher Pittman, 12, committed a killing at home while on Paxil and Zoloft on November 28, 2001.

Cory Baadsgaard, 16, was imprisoned under the influence of Paxil/Seroxat and Effexor on April 15, 2001.

Additional incidents include Vickie McCarthy's Paxil withdrawal leading to electrical zaps and a suicide attempt on August 27, 2004, as reported by Omaha Channel.

The Ledger Report on January 1, 2004, linked Paxil/Seroxat (paroxetine) to a crash.

Alicia Quartermain, 18, engaged in self-harm due to Paxil/Seroxat/Aropax (paroxetine) in August 2003.

Michelle van Syckel, as reported by the Boston Globe on August 5, 2003, experienced suicidal tendencies while on Seroxat/Paxil.

Novelist Helen Walsh, as reported by The Guardian on June 12, 2003, was suicidal during her time on Seroxat/Paxil.

Colin Whitfield, 56, committed suicide linked to Seroxat/Paxil on June 1, 2003.

Douglas Bruce Hopey, whose suicide in December 2001 was linked to Paxil/Seroxat (paroxetine).

Kara Jaye-Anne Otter, only 12 years old, tragically committed suicide while on Paxil/Seroxat, as reported in June 2001.

One potential side effect of psychiatric medications is heightened mental activity, restlessness, and agitation, which can precipitate violent ideation and behavior. These medications function by slowing cognitive processing in the higher brain regions, impairing the patient's ability to engage in deliberate reasoning that could otherwise moderate intense emotional responses such as fear, anger, or revenge. Consequently, actions may occur without the typical inhibitory control of higher cognitive functions.

Careful consideration is warranted regarding the prescription of such medications, particularly those associated with heightened aggression. Their administration should be reserved for severe psychiatric conditions under the supervision of healthcare professionals, rather than prescribed casually for mild depression under the guise of safety. The profound risk of violence linked to these drugs is substantial, encompassing tragic events like shooting sprees, domestic violence, and numerous suicides (Mass murder and psychiatric drugs, n.d.).

David Carmichael's harrowing experience serves as a poignant cautionary tale for Canadians about the importance of understanding pharmaceutical effects. Although not widely recognized, Carmichael gained notoriety in 2004 when he faced charges of first-degree murder following the death of his 11-year-old son, Ian. Convinced that his son, who had a mild form of epilepsy, posed a danger due to perceived brain damage, Carmichael administered sedatives and subsequently strangled him during a father-son weekend in London, Ontario. After the act, Carmichael recounted kissing his son goodbye, expressing love, and then spending hours watching television before notifying authorities (Prescription drug side-effects: How they're vastly under-reported and one man's tragic, cautionary tale, 2021).

During his trial, Carmichael was diagnosed with psychotic depression and ultimately deemed not criminally responsible, receiving treatment at a psychiatric facility in Eastern Ontario for four years. His case underscores the potential triggering effects of antidepressants such as Paxil, which his wife Beth believes precipitated his psychosis, irreversibly altering their family's life.

The manufacturer's warning for Paxil acknowledges the drug's potential to induce severe agitation and pose risks of self-harm or harm to others. Health Canada reported 258 serious adverse reactions associated with Paxil since Ian's tragic death, including suicides, suicidal thoughts or attempts, and incidents of homicidal ideation or violence (Prescription drug side-effects: How they're vastly under-reported and one man's tragic, cautionary tale, 2021).

Since 2019, Canadian acute care hospitals have been mandated to report all adverse drug reactions to Health Canada. Initial data revealed a 300% increase in reports over previous periods, though underreporting remains a recognized issue within both voluntary and mandatory surveillance systems (Prescription drug side-effects: How they're vastly under-reported and one man's tragic, cautionary tale, 2021).

David Carmichael has since embarked on a nationwide speaking tour to share his family's devastating experience, urging Canadians to report adverse reactions and conduct thorough research before taking medications. His advocacy aims to prevent similar tragedies and contribute to public awareness and accountability (Prescription drug side-effects: How they're vastly under-reported and one man's tragic, cautionary tale, 2021).

Recent revelations from the Veterans Health Administration shed light on the case of Micah Johnson, an Army reservist suffering from post-traumatic stress disorder (PTSD) following his return from Afghanistan in 2014. Despite exhibiting symptoms such as anxiety, depression, and hallucinations—including nightmares and auditory hallucinations of war—the healthcare providers concluded he did not pose a significant risk to himself or others. This assessment was based on documentation obtained through the Freedom of Information Act (Army reservist who killed 5 Dallas officers showed symptoms of PTSD, 2016).

Tragically, Johnson went on to perpetrate the fatal shooting of five Dallas police officers during a peaceful protest in 2016. Armed with an assault rifle, he strategically positioned himself to attack officers, leading to a standoff resolved by law enforcement's use of a bomb-carrying robot (Army reservist who killed 5 Dallas officers showed symptoms of PTSD, 2016).

During his deployment, Johnson's experiences in Afghanistan, though in a previously intense combat zone, did not prepare him for the resurgence of trauma upon his return to civilian life. His documented panic attacks and acute distress in public places underscore the severe impact of untreated PTSD on veterans (Army reservist who killed 5 Dallas officers showed symptoms of PTSD, 2016).

Veteran stated that the cacophony of noises, altercations, and police interventions triggered palpitations, as documented in the records: "My heart felt like someone was pinching it while it was beating rapidly" (Army reservist who killed 5 Dallas officers showed symptoms of PTSD, 2016). Johnson reported subsequent shaking, shortness of breath, and chills following the Walmart incident. The records do not indicate a formal PTSD diagnosis for Johnson. The screening he underwent typically serves as an initial step to determine referral to mental health professionals, according to Joel Dvoskin, a clinical and forensic psychologist in Tucson, Arizona.

Physicians eventually assessed Johnson as presenting a low suicide risk and no immediate threat to others. Medical records from August 15, 2014, note that Johnson was "not acutely at risk for harm to self or others" and was not observed to be psychotic.

The reservist, specializing in carpentry and masonry, reported lower back pain and anxiety in crowds, habitually scanning for exits and observing others' behaviors in public. "I feel like I can't trust all of these strangers around me," Johnson conveyed to his doctor, noting increased anger and irritability since returning to Dallas, where he admitted to consuming three to four shots of vodka, up to three times a week.

During a visit on August 15, records indicate Johnson described his childhood as "stressful." His responses regarding abuse history were redacted. Johnson also raised concerns about erectile dysfunction and was advised to consult with a healthcare provider. He was prescribed a muscle relaxant, antidepressant, anti-anxiety medication, and sleep aids. A nurse provided anger management tips. Johnson underwent further evaluation for PTSD symptoms by a psychiatrist in September 2014, with noted improvement in mood.

In October 2014, Johnson deferred further PTSD assessment, citing home remodeling obligations. Previously, he expressed plans to pursue construction work and long-term aspirations to become a self-defense instructor.

Delphene Johnson, his mother, reported that her son sought VA medical care for a back injury but faced obstacles with paperwork and meetings, ultimately feeling unsupported by the system. Dallas VA representatives did not respond to inquiries regarding Johnson's treatment within the VA North Texas Health Care System, one of the largest in the country.

In May 2014, new mental health patients at the Dallas VA experienced an average 50-day wait, among the longest in the nation at the time. The mother of Gavin Long, another veteran involved in a fatal shooting incident, highlighted his PTSD struggles and challenges in accessing VA assistance (Army reservist who killed 5 Dallas officers showed symptoms of PTSD, 2016).

This case bears striking resemblance to that of Juan David Ortiz. Notably, research into the effectiveness of paroxetine, a serotonin-reuptake inhibitor combined with cognitive-behavioral therapy, in treating problematic pornography use (PPU) was conducted. Three heterosexual males received this treatment, with assessments revealing initial reductions in pornography consumption and anxiety. However, after three months, patients exhibited new compulsive sexual behaviors. Patients A and C engaged in paid sexual relations multiple times weekly, and Patient B began an extramarital affair. Patient C even extended his involvement to a two-week vacation. These emerging behaviors were discussed during follow-up sessions, with Patients A and B grappling with moral conflicts due to their strong religious convictions (Paroxetine treatment of problematic pornography use: A case series, 2016).

In a separate legal matter, SmithKline Beecham, a manufacturer of a leading antidepressant, was ordered to pay $8 million in damages to the relatives of a man who committed suicide and killed others after taking Paxil. The jury found Paxil culpable for causing suicidal and homicidal tendencies, leading to the deaths of multiple individuals, including Donald Schell and his family members (SmithKline Beecham to pay $8 million, 1998).

Veteran Johnson recounted experiencing palpitations induced by the cacophony of noises, altercations, and police interventions, stating, "My heart felt like someone was pinching it while it was beating fast" (Army reservist who killed 5 Dallas officers showed symptoms of PTSD, 2016). Following the Walmart incident, Johnson reported shaking, shortness of breath, and chills. Despite not being formally diagnosed with PTSD, his initial screening served as a preliminary assessment to determine the need for further mental health evaluation, as explained by Joel Dvoskin, a clinical and forensic psychologist in Tucson, Arizona.

Medical assessments eventually concluded that Johnson posed a low risk for suicide or harm to others. According to records dated August 15, 2014, Johnson was deemed "not acutely at risk for harm to self or others," and showed no signs of psychosis. The reservist, skilled in carpentry and masonry, disclosed to healthcare providers his struggles with lower back pain and avoidance of crowds, habitually scanning for exits and monitoring individuals' actions in public settings.

Johnson expressed difficulty in trusting strangers and feelings of anger and irritability, exacerbated by his consumption of three to four shots of vodka up to three times weekly since returning to Dallas. Records from an August 15 visit indicate that Johnson described his childhood as "stressful," with redacted responses regarding his history of abuse. He also raised concerns about erectile dysfunction during consultations, leading to prescriptions for muscle relaxants, antidepressants, anti-anxiety medications, and sleep aids, alongside counseling on anger management. Subsequent evaluations in September of that year noted improvement in his mood following psychiatric intervention.

During a follow-up call in October 2014, Johnson postponed further PTSD assessments due to ongoing house remodeling obligations. He had earlier expressed intentions to pursue a career in construction and aspire to become a self-defense instructor. Johnson's mother, Delphene Johnson, recounted his frustrations with obtaining adequate medical care from the VA for a back injury, which ultimately led him to "just finally give up," according to The Blaze.

In May 2014, new patients seeking mental health care at the Dallas VA faced a 50-day average wait, underscoring systemic challenges in timely access to treatment. Similarly, the mother of Gavin Long, the former Marine and Iraq war veteran who fatally shot three law enforcement officers in Baton Rouge on July 17, stated that her son, suffering from PTSD, sought but did not receive sufficient help from the VA (Army reservist who killed 5 Dallas officers showed symptoms of PTSD, 2016).

This case shares notable parallels with that of Juan David Ortiz. Both instances highlight systemic issues in veterans' mental health care and the challenges in accessing timely and appropriate treatment.

A study investigating the efficacy of the serotonin-reuptake inhibitor paroxetine, combined with cognitive-behavioral therapy, in treating problematic pornography use (PPU) involved three heterosexual males. Although initial findings suggested paroxetine's effectiveness in reducing PPU and associated anxiety, it was linked to the emergence of new compulsive sexual behaviors after three months of treatment. Notably, within 12-14 weeks, Patients A and C engaged in paid sexual relations up to three times weekly, while Patient B initiated an extramarital affair with his children's caregiver. Patients A and B, driven by strong religious beliefs, viewed extramarital affairs as morally reprehensible, highlighting the complex interplay of moral values and compulsive behaviors in treatment outcomes ("Paroxetine treatment of problematic pornography use: A case series," 2016).

In a legal context, the manufacturer of the nation's second-best-selling antidepressant, Paxil, was ordered to pay $8 million to the relatives of a man who tragically killed himself and three others after consuming the drug. The jury's verdict in the wrongful death civil suit underscored Paxil's potential to induce suicidal or homicidal behaviors, affirming it as a contributing factor in the deaths (Army reservist who killed 5 Dallas officers showed symptoms of PTSD, 2016).

This narrative exemplifies the critical intersections of mental health care, pharmaceutical treatments, and legal accountability in cases involving psychiatric medications.

The jury attributed 80 percent of the fault in the case to the drug manufacturer and 20 percent to Donald Schell. A call seeking comment from representatives of the pharmaceutical company was not immediately returned today. In his closing arguments, Vickery stated that Paxil can induce suicidal and homicidal reactions in a small subset of individuals. "Since 1990, SmithKline Beecham knew there was a small group at risk, and Don Schell was one of those vulnerable people," he asserted. The company, now GlaxoSmithKline PLC, failed to provide adequate warnings on the label regarding the potential for violent reactions and did not sufficiently test for the risk of such reactions (ABC News, 2001).

A U.S. jury in Wyoming found the British-based pharmaceutical company GlaxoSmithKline responsible for a series of family murders and a suicide committed by a patient taking the antidepressant paroxetine, marketed as Paxil in the United States and Seroxat in the United Kingdom. Mr. Schell reportedly suffered from episodic depression but had not exhibited suicidal or homicidal ideation or violent behavior prior to being prescribed paroxetine, an antidepressant of the selective serotonin reuptake inhibitor class. Several years earlier, he had been prescribed fluoxetine (Prozac), a related drug, but was taken off it due to extreme agitation.

In February 1998, he was prescribed paroxetine for mild depression, and within weeks he went on a murderous rampage. The jury concluded that the drug was 80% responsible for the four deaths. The Wyoming decision marked the first instance in which a pharmaceutical company was held liable for the suicidal or homicidal actions of an individual taking its antidepressant. The jury's verdict re-ignites concerns over the safety of selective serotonin reuptake inhibitors and their possible association with violent behavior, dealing a serious blow to manufacturers of this popular class of antidepressants, which also includes fluoxetine and sertraline.

Selective serotonin reuptake inhibitors, introduced in the late 1980s and early 1990s, quickly supplanted tricyclic antidepressants and monoamine oxidase inhibitors as the preferred treatment for depression. However, soon after their introduction, reports of paradoxical reactions, including mania, psychosis, restlessness, and increased suicidal ideation, began to surface. Fluoxetine, the first selective serotonin reuptake inhibitor, received significant negative press. In the early 1990s, several lawsuits were brought against Eli Lilly, the maker of fluoxetine, alleging that the medication caused aggressive behavior in a subset of patients. These suits were either settled out of court, dismissed, or won by the pharmaceutical company. The negative publicity prompted Eli Lilly to issue a "Dear Doctor" letter on August 31, 1990, to reassure physicians that no causal relationship existed between increased suicidal tendencies and fluoxetine.

Selective serotonin reuptake inhibitors are generally considered safe and effective, but they can cause akathisia, or excessive internal restlessness, in a subset of patients. This akathisia is believed to contribute to subsequent violent behavior. In reaching its decision, the jury considered literature on selective serotonin reuptake inhibitors and the testimony of David Healy, Director of Psychological Medicine in Bangor, North Wales. Dr. Healy served as an expert witness for the plaintiffs and testified that both his research and that of GlaxoSmithKline indicated that up to 25% of previously healthy volunteers who took selective serotonin reuptake inhibitors became extremely agitated (Josefson, 2001).

In his small studies of this class of antidepressants, conducted with non-depressed volunteers given sertraline, Dr. Healy found that 33% felt better on the drug, 33% felt worse, and 33% did not respond at all. Two previously non-suicidal and non-depressed volunteers became suicidal and depressed while on the drug. Historically, patients in the early stages of recovery from depression, especially "vegetative depression," have a slightly increased risk of suicide because antidepressants provide them with more energy to carry out suicidal plans (Josefson, 2001).

Jake Steinberg had bitten his nails since childhood, but when a doctor noticed the California college student's anxious habit, he prescribed Paxil. "It was a terrible mistake," his father, Robert Steinberg, told The Post. Just over a month later, Jake, a talented glee-club singer, music composer, and student newspaper editor, began acting bizarrely during his summer internship at the prestigious William Morris Agency in Manhattan. On July 23, 2003, Jake smashed a chair through a window on the 24th floor of 1325 Sixth Ave. and jumped to his death. The shocking suicide was a mystery, as the outgoing, ever-smiling redhead was the last person his friends and family thought would kill himself. "It was so out of character," his father said. "He was in love with life. He couldn't wait for the next day to make his next plan."

Jake's parents now contend that Paxil, prescribed for depression and anxiety to millions of children, teens, and adults, caused the psychotic behavior that led to his senseless suicide. "We feel very strongly that Paxil caused his death," Robert Steinberg stated. He believes that he and other doctors were unaware of Paxil's dangers. Jake's restlessness, they have since learned, can be a symptom of akathisia—excessive movement, a common side effect of psychiatric drugs. "It's like you're on fire, and you can't sit still. You just want to do anything to get out of the torment," his father explained. The couple is outraged that Paxil and other antidepressants could be prescribed so loosely, and they are hopeful that Jake's story will spur stronger warnings. "We can't bring Jake back, but it's something that should never happen to another family," his father concluded (Edelman, 2004).

Paxil, an antidepressant medication introduced in 1992, functions as a selective serotonin reuptake inhibitor (SSRI) used to treat various mental health conditions, including depression, social anxiety, panic disorders, and phobias.

One significant adverse effect associated with Paxil is an increase in suicidal behaviors. Since 2005, numerous lawsuits have been filed against GlaxoSmithKline, the pharmaceutical company that manufactures Paxil, alleging that the company concealed or misrepresented information regarding these potential side effects. Consequently, individuals claim to have suffered harm, injury, or death due to Paxil usage. Thus, the question arises: Can Paxil, purportedly an antidepressant, contribute to fatal outcomes? The answer, distressingly, is affirmative. Paxil can profoundly impact one's life, causing injury, harm, birth defects, and even death (Johnson Law Group, n.d.).

Paxil is also associated with other severe side effects. It is crucial to report to your physician if you:

- Experience suicidal thoughts

- Develop new or worsened depression

- Exhibit aggressive or violent behavior

- Struggle with insomnia

- Feel restless

- Suffer from new or exacerbated anxiety and panic attacks

- Notice unusual behavioral or mood changes

Additionally, the combination of alcohol and paroxetine can amplify certain adverse effects, including:

- Drowsiness

- Impaired judgment

- Sleepiness

- Hallucinations

- Hypertension

- Irregular heart rhythm

- Restlessness

- Muscle stiffness

- Nausea

- Vomiting

- Sexual dysfunction

- Weight gain

- Joint pain

- Paranoia

- Suicidal ideation (Wooldridge, 2023).

Dr. David Healy, who accessed GlaxoSmithKline's archives during the Schell trial in Cheyenne, Wyoming, provided crucial insights into the potential risks associated with Paxil. Tim Tobin, the son-in-law of Donald Schell, whose wife and child died, along with other family members, sued GlaxoSmithKline, alleging a violent reaction to Paxil (Seroxat).

During the trial, it emerged that 34 studies involving healthy volunteer company workers, conducted before Paxil's licensing, showed that 25% became agitated while taking the medication. Dr. Healy suggested that a minority might become disturbed enough by SSRI effects to harm themselves or others.

Notably, these studies were conducted by general hospital doctors interested in gastrointestinal disorders, not psychiatrists who might have probed deeper into mental health issues in otherwise healthy individuals. Although Dr. Healy was supposed to review all studies, four conducted by psychiatrists were missing. One psychiatrist's note revealed an unusually high incidence of problems in healthy volunteers. Dr. Healy claims to have examined all available pre-licensing healthy volunteer studies, except for inexplicably missing material. In a March deposition, GlaxoSmithKline admitted that he had reviewed a representative sample.

Dr. Healy conveyed his concerns about these studies to the UK's Medicines Control Agency, which issues drug licenses. He mentioned that some volunteers subsequently engaged in suicidal behavior, indicating a troubling link between paroxetine intake and later suicidal acts.

GlaxoSmithKline denies that its drug can provoke murder or suicide, or cause withdrawal problems. Dr. Healy rebuts this, stating that withdrawal symptoms such as agitation, insomnia, or abnormal dreams in healthy volunteers without prior depression are clearly drug-induced (Boseley, 2001).

It's worth noting that while Juan David Ortiz, a former Border Patrol agent, was prescribed Paxil by the Veterans Affairs (VA) hospital, this medication was not directly linked to his legal case. His situation underscores ongoing concerns about the safety and potential risks associated with Paxil, especially when prescribed without adequate monitoring or follow-up.

Juan David Ortiz reported the following medications for various conditions: Paxil for depression, divalproex sodium for irritability, trazodone for insomnia, and gabapentin for migraine headaches. Although the Veterans Affairs (VA) doctor increased the dosages, Ortiz could not recall the specific dates of these adjustments. He began taking these medications in mid-February and continued until his arrest.

Ortiz began soliciting prostitutes approximately five months before his arrest, around mid-May. It took him between two to three months from the start of his medication regimen to begin engaging with sex workers. Prior to taking these medications, Ortiz had not sought the services of prostitutes.

CHAPTER 9
THE DEATH PENALTY

Juan David Ortiz, a war veteran who served in Iraq, does not deserve the death penalty. His service to the country, coupled with the mental health issues he developed from the trauma of war, warrants our compassion and support, not capital punishment. The death penalty is fundamentally flawed and unjust.

The death penalty in the United States is experiencing a significant decline in both usage and public support. According to an annual report on capital punishment, many Americans now believe that the death penalty is administered unfairly. This growing sentiment is contributing to its increasing isolation within the U.S. However, the ultimate abolition of capital punishment remains uncertain, as experts are divided on whether the public's waning support and the decreasing number of executions and death sentences will lead to its complete eradication.

In 2023, there were 24 executions in the United States, with the final one occurring in Oklahoma. Additionally, 21 individuals were sentenced to death that year, marking the ninth consecutive year with fewer than 30 executions and fewer than 50 death sentences, according to the Death Penalty Information Center. Only five states—Texas, Florida, Missouri, Oklahoma, and Alabama—conducted executions in 2023, the lowest number in 20 years. This trend underscores the increasing isolation of the death penalty in the U.S.

A Gallup poll from October revealed that 50% of Americans believe capital punishment is applied unfairly, while 47% believe it is justly administered. This is the highest percentage of skepticism since Gallup began surveying the legitimacy of the death penalty's application in 2000. The shift in public opinion may be linked to the increased scrutiny of the U.S. criminal justice system, particularly following the 2020 killing of George Floyd by a police officer.

Nearly 200 death row exonerations since 1975, including three in 2023, have also influenced public perceptions of the death penalty's fairness. Various individuals, including conservative legislators, have expressed concerns about or debated the future of capital punishment. Nonetheless, in states like Alabama, Florida, Oklahoma, and Texas, the death penalty remains deeply entrenched.

Earlier this year, Florida Governor Ron DeSantis signed bills enacting two new death penalty laws. One permits the death penalty in child rape convictions, despite a U.S. Supreme Court ruling prohibiting capital punishment in such cases. The other law eliminates the requirement for a unanimous jury in death penalty sentencing. "If you commit a heinous crime, you should receive the ultimate punishment," DeSantis stated in May regarding the death penalty for child rape convictions.

The ongoing difficulties in securing supplies of execution drugs have led some states to explore new and untested methods of execution or to revive previously abandoned ones. Alabama has scheduled a January execution using nitrogen gas, the nation's first attempt at this method. In July, Idaho became the fifth state to authorize executions by firing squad, a method last used in the U.S. in 2010. Currently, 29 states have either abolished the death penalty or paused executions.

The number of states without the death penalty could potentially rise to 40. However, a nationwide ban would require action from the U.S. Supreme Court, which appears unlikely given its recent decisions. The Supreme Court granted only one stay of execution out of 34 requests made during its 2022-23 term.

Texas, the nation's busiest capital punishment state, has not been immune to the ongoing debate. Earlier this year, the GOP-led Texas House passed a bill to eliminate the death penalty in cases involving individuals diagnosed with schizophrenia. The bill, however, failed as it was never considered by the Texas Senate. GOP state Representative Jeff Leach stated in March that the bill was not an effort to abolish the death penalty in Texas. "I believe that Texas needs the death penalty," Leach said. "But as a supporter of the death penalty, I oppose executing individuals who were severely mentally ill at the time of their offense."

While there may be some changes to the death penalty in Texas, a complete abolition of capital punishment remains unlikely at this time.

As a Catholic, I oppose the death penalty. The Bible explicitly commands, "Thou shall not kill."

Ortiz, a veteran who served our country, fought in Iraq for our freedom, and worked as a federal agent for most of his life, has no prior criminal history. He suffers from PTSD, TBI, and possibly other war-related mental health issues, and was suicidal. We send our men to war, train them to kill, and then neglect their mental health needs when they return.

Execution is not a solution to deter violence. According to the National Research Council of the National Academies of Sciences, all existing studies on the death penalty's deterrent effect are methodologically flawed and unreliable. The death penalty cannot be justified as a necessary public safety measure, as it has not been proven to reduce crime. While reasonable individuals might be deterred from committing a crime by the threat of execution, those who commit murder rarely act rationally at the time of their offense.

Research consistently shows that the death penalty does not deter criminals from committing either premeditated or impulsive crimes. States that retain the death penalty tend to have higher murder rates than the national average, according to FBI data.

The Death Penalty: An Ineffective and Costly Measure

Numerous countries, such as Canada, that have abolished the death penalty have experienced a decline in violent crime rates. The Death Penalty Information Center has reported that police chiefs rank the death penalty last among methods to reduce violent crime. These law enforcement leaders also consider it the least efficient use of taxpayers' money.

The use of the death penalty hinders the search for effective solutions to violent crime by providing a false sense of security. Moreover, it could be argued that capital punishment increases societal brutality, perpetuating a cycle of violence. As a society, we fail if our only response to those affected by violent acts is more violence and death.

Assertion: "The death penalty is demanded by and carried out in the name of the victims' families."

Refutation: Punishment for a crime should not be determined by the victim's family's desires, as this would result in arbitrary sentencing, reflecting disparate notions of justice from case to case. Ideally, a justice system should impose consistent penalties for criminal acts. While it is natural to feel anger and frustration over the loss of innocent lives due to murder, it is crucial to recognize that not all victims' families support capital punishment. Many families of victims oppose the death penalty.

Capital punishment itself creates additional victims—the family members of the executed individual—and can severely impact the prison officials tasked with carrying out executions. Although it may be assumed that the severity of the crime and the culpability of the offender are the main determinants of execution, evidence suggests otherwise. Local politics, the quality of legal counsel, the location of the crime, plea bargaining, and chance significantly influence death sentencing in the United States. Offenders who commit similar crimes under comparable circumstances often receive vastly different sentences. The race of both the offender and the victim, as well as socioeconomic status, play significant roles in determining who lives and who dies (Texas Coalition to Abolish the Death Penalty).

Inadequate legal representation, unreliable expert testimony, and community biases frequently affect verdicts and sentencing. In Texas, district attorneys are elected officials, and some seek the death penalty more frequently than others due to personal inclinations or political pressures. Their decisions often depend on whether they believe a jury will deliver a death sentence and the associated costs.

Assertion: "I don't want my tax dollars to go toward incarcerating convicted murderers."

Refutation: The costs associated with the death penalty far exceed those of life imprisonment. The greatest expenses are incurred before and during the trial, not in post-conviction proceedings. Even if all appeals were eliminated, the death penalty system would remain more costly than alternative sentences. In Texas, county taxpayers must fund expensive death penalty trials and automatic appeals, along with any resentencing hearings or retrials. Executing a person in Texas costs two to three times more than imprisoning someone for life. Some counties spend so much on seeking the death penalty that they must cut law enforcement funding and raise taxes (Texas Coalition to Abolish the Death Penalty).

Assertion: "The American justice system is the best in the world and offers proper safeguards against mistakes."

Refutation: While many Americans trust the justice system, the possibility of errors should prompt reconsideration of the "justice" involved in pursuing the death penalty. Despite the system's merits, it is based on human judgment and is susceptible to mistakes. Consequently, the risk of executing an innocent person always exists. Factors such as false testimony from jailhouse informants, mistaken eyewitness identification, evidence misinterpretation, incompetent legal representation, unreliable expert testimony, and community biases frequently impact verdicts and sentencing.

Since 1973, 138 individuals have been released from death row due to credible evidence of wrongful conviction, including 12 in Texas. DNA evidence was pivotal in establishing innocence in only 17 of these cases. Many exonerations resulted from the dedicated efforts of journalism students, lawyers, and activists rather than the justice system itself. Investigations into several Texas cases suggest that innocent people may have been executed (Texas Coalition to Abolish the Death Penalty).

Pursuing the death penalty extends the duration and cost of legal proceedings, often without resulting in execution. The average cost of a death penalty case in Texas is $2.3 million, approximately three times the cost of imprisoning someone in a high-security cell for 40 years. Housing an inmate in Texas prisons costs $47.50 per day, totaling over $17,000 annually and $693,500 for 40 years.

The financial burden is even more significant for smaller counties. For instance, Jasper County, Texas, raised property taxes by nearly 7% to fund a single death penalty case. The excessive costs persist through the appeals process, as counties must pay for both trials and state appeals, along with any resentencing hearings or retrials. Some counties allocate so many resources to pursuing the death penalty that they must reduce funding for law enforcement and raise taxes (Texas Coalition to Abolish the Death Penalty).

Both Dennis Rader, infamously known as the BTK serial killer in Kansas, and Gary Ridgeway, the Washington state man who confessed to committing 48 murders over 20 years, received life sentences for their heinous crimes. Eddie Ray Routh faced a death penalty-eligible charge following the February 2, 2013, shooting deaths of former Navy SEAL Chris Kyle, known as the "American Sniper," aged 38, and veteran Chad Littlefield, aged 35. Routh took the lives of two heroes, one of whom was a legend. Nevertheless, Erath County District Attorney Alan Nash sought a life-without-parole sentence for Routh instead of the death penalty. Routh's history of military service may have influenced the prosecutors' decision, as they likely anticipated that jurors would be reluctant to condemn a troubled veteran to death row. *American Sniper*, the film based on Kyle's account of his experiences as a Navy SEAL, was nominated for Best Picture at the Oscars.

Gabriel Cardona, who was already incarcerated on murder and kidnapping charges, managed to make bail twice, enabling him to go on two killing sprees under the orders of a leader of the Gulf drug-smuggling cartel in Nuevo Laredo. Cardona was arrested on April 12, 2006, and charged with two counts of murder, bringing the total number of murder charges to five. He also faced multiple other offenses, ranging from aggravated assault to organized crime. In February, Cardona accepted a plea agreement for the murders of Orozco and Lopez. He was sentenced by a new judge to 50 years in prison, making him eligible for parole in 25 years.

It is crucial to examine capital punishment on a systemic level, rather than solely through the lens of the most gruesome and reprehensible cases. When proponents assert that the death penalty is just and that certain individuals deserve death as punishment, they often overlook the complexities and potential inequities inherent in the system. Approximately two percent of those eligible for the death penalty receive death sentences in the United States, and far less than one percent are ultimately executed, according to the Texas Coalition to Abolish the Death Penalty. The death penalty is not notably effective in its implementation and imposes a significant financial burden on taxpayers.

LAREDO'S HISTORY OF THE DEATH PENALTY

Arturo Aranda has languished on death row for nearly five decades. Convicted of fatally shooting a law enforcement officer in Laredo, Texas, on July 31, 1976, he was sentenced to death on May 18, 1979.

Rogelio Hernandez, convicted of capital murder for the slaying of Officer Jose Herrera during an attempted escape from the Webb County Jail on February 3, 1986, also faced the ultimate penalty.

"Rogelio Hernandez succumbed to a heart attack in prison. As lead counsel, I achieved a rare reversal on appeal in death penalty cases. The Court of Criminal Appeals overturned his conviction and death sentence, after which I withdrew as his attorney due to his claims of my ineffective counsel during the appeal. Despite winning the appeal, I refused to continue representing him. Charlie Borchers, a former District Attorney in Webb County, replaced me, and Hernandez was once again sentenced to death. Although Borchers appealed, he was unsuccessful. The protracted appeals process ultimately prevented the state from executing Hernandez," recounted Attorney Eduardo Peña.

Miguel Angel Martinez, implicated in the notorious "Smiley" case, received a death sentence in 1991. Following extensive appeals, his sentence was commuted to life imprisonment in 2002.

Demond Bluntson remains on death row since 2016 and is currently pursuing an appeal.

On July 18, 2023, after approximately nine hours of deliberation, a Texas jury sentenced former Supervisory United States Border Patrol Agent Ronald Anthony Burgos-Aviles, aged 34, to life without parole instead of the death penalty for the 2018 double murder of Grizelda Hernandez, aged 27, and their one-year-old son, Dominic Alexander. This verdict, rendered in Texas—a state with the highest execution rate since 1976—reflects a shifting attitude toward the death penalty. The number of new death sentences in Texas has significantly decreased from a peak of 51 in 1999 to just 2 in 2022. Similarly, the number of executions has dropped from 40 in 2000 to 5 in 2022 (Death Penalty Information Center, 2022).

California Governor Gavin Newsom's executive order has established an immediate moratorium on executions, citing the immorality of state-sanctioned killing. "The intentional killing of another person is wrong," Governor Newsom stated. "As governor, I will not oversee the execution of any individual." This order provides an immediate reprieve for all death row inmates and exemplifies the governor's executive power to commute death sentences. Unlike the usual practice of individual commutations, this order implements a blanket moratorium. Governors in Oregon, Colorado, and Pennsylvania have enacted similar measures. Newsom has long opposed the death penalty, criticizing it as a "failed policy" that is both costly and fundamentally immoral.

Newsom's administration has highlighted several reasons for this moratorium, including the death penalty's inherent racial and mental health biases, the irreversible risk of wrongful executions, and the excessive financial burden without any demonstrable increase in public safety. "The death penalty has provided no public safety benefit or value as a deterrent. It has wasted billions of taxpayer dollars. But most of all, the death penalty is absolute—irreversible and irreparable in the event of human error," Newsom asserted.

Several prominent Democratic leaders, including Vice President Kamala Harris and Senator Bernie Sanders, advocate for the abolition of the death penalty. In contrast, former President Donald Trump has endorsed capital punishment for drug dealers and those who murder police officers. Pope Francis has also condemned the death penalty, declaring it "inadmissible" and an affront to human dignity, urging the Catholic Church to strive for its global abolition.

Approximately 15-20% of Texas death row inmates receive ongoing mental health services. The "insanity defense" is infrequently employed and even less frequently successful, with fewer than one percent of defendants raising it and an even smaller fraction being found not guilty by reason of insanity (Psychiatric Times, 2022).

The American Bar Association, American Psychiatric Association, American Psychological Association, and National Alliance on Mental Illness have all recommended prohibiting the death penalty for individuals with severe mental disorders or disabilities. Numerous mental health organizations in Texas have also condemned the execution of offenders with severe mental illnesses.

CHAPTER 10
JUAN DAVID ORTIZ'S TRUTH

Juan David Ortiz (Ortiz) is currently appealing his case. The primary consideration is whether the District Attorney (DA) should have sent a war veteran to death row. Ortiz, a medic who saved lives in Iraq, tragically took four lives in Laredo, Texas, due to the influence of Paxil medication and Post-Traumatic Stress Disorder (PTSD).

On January 25, 2022, District Attorney Alaniz convened a meeting with 1-2 representatives from each of the victims' families. Present were the Assistant DA and two deputies working for DA Alaniz. This conference, held in the Central Courtroom on the third floor of the Justice Center, aimed to confirm whether the families still wished to pursue the death penalty. The families initially agreed, but Joey Cantu, one of the family representatives, requested to speak. His statement influenced the families, leading them to change their stance and opt for life imprisonment without the possibility of parole.

Joey Cantu's impact statement, recorded on video, included a plea to DA Alaniz to consider life imprisonment without parole. The victims' families later publicly acknowledged DA Alaniz's efforts: "DA Alaniz and his team accomplished their goals. DA Alaniz fulfilled his duty and secured the justice the families sought."

Webb County District Attorney Isidro R. "Chilo" Alaniz was invited to present the case study of Juan David Ortiz, the supervisory Border Patrol agent turned serial killer, at the *Texas District and County Attorneys Association Annual Investigator Conference* in San Marcos. Alaniz will share strategies, techniques, and insights into the preparation, prosecution, and conviction of Ortiz with approximately 500 criminal investigators.

"This case was the first in Webb County's history to be tried before a Bexar County jury in San Antonio, Texas, commonly known as *Military City USA*. Ortiz, a Navy medic and Iraq veteran, faced a strong defense team from San Antonio. We had to present the case at the Bexar County Courthouse to a San Antonio jury," stated Alaniz. The defense argued that Ortiz's PTSD diminished his mental capacity, aiming for jury nullification by appealing to the empathy of one or two jurors.

If discussing this case with the media, it is crucial to be well-informed and factual. National media should consult reliable sources to avoid spreading misinformation. Authentic and accurate information is vital for representing Laredo, Texas, accurately. Many aspire to gain notoriety by claiming to have broken the case or compelled Ortiz to speak. Only subject matter experts with detailed knowledge should comment on the case. Books written by outsiders about Ortiz lack the exclusive information I have directly from him. Ortiz is not giving interviews and is currently appealing his case. It is unjust that people exploit Ortiz for fame, treating him like a spectacle. He is a person, a human being.

I harbor no hatred towards Ortiz; judgment is between him and God. Observing Ortiz's transformation from a civilian to a convict in the confession video was poignant. He changed from a normal human being to a prisoner, losing his freedom in an instant. It was heartbreaking to witness the transformation of a man who had been good for most of his life but then succumbed to a dark path.

For four to five months, Ortiz frequented sex workers before snapping. Ortiz is a good person who committed terrible acts. Engaging with prostitutes is an ancient profession, mentioned even in biblical times. Ortiz loves his children and was likely a good father, but the combination of sex, PTSD, and Paxil medication altered his personality. The drug Paxil changed him into someone else.

Ortiz should have pursued a divorce, sought marriage therapy, and started a new relationship with someone compatible with his intelligence if his marital sex life was unsatisfying. Divorce is not the end; it can be a new beginning.

Ortiz's actions were becoming increasingly reckless. He left bullet casings and frequented the same locations with the same truck, leaving bodies nearby. Eventually, law enforcement would have caught him during surveillance of the areas where the bodies were found. An undercover female agent posing as a sex worker with a tracking device could have entrapped him. Ortiz's case gained significant media attention nationwide, reflecting its notoriety.

To address both sides of the issue, Ortiz required better medication and therapy for his PTSD and Traumatic Brain Injury (TBI). A judge should mandate rehabilitation instead of incarceration and ensure individuals receive medication for controlling HIV, AIDS, and Hepatitis C.

Jesus forgave Saint Paul despite his persecution of Christians.

God used St. Paul as His instrument to carry His name. Saint Paul is an example that anyone, even the most hardened unbeliever or the vilest heretic, can be created anew by our loving Savior. Some might say that one of Paul's weaknesses was that he was a very stubborn and strong-minded man. —*Acts 16:36 - 41*

It may just be that Paul was such a man, but God took this energy and determination and used it for His glory in the widespread dissemination of the Gospel. Once Paul set his mind to do a thing, only the direct intervention of the Holy Spirit could stop him. —*Acts 16:16*

Dr. Martin Luther King Jr. eloquently expressed the inherent flaw of violence: "The ultimate weakness of violence is that it is a descending spiral, begetting the very thing it seeks to destroy. Instead of diminishing evil, it multiplies it. Through violence, you may murder the liar, but you cannot murder the lie, nor establish the truth. Through violence, you may murder the hater, but you do not murder hate. Violence merely increases hate. So, it goes. Returning violence for violence multiplies violence, adding deeper darkness to a night already devoid of stars. Darkness cannot drive out darkness: only light can do that. Hate cannot drive out hate: only love can do that."

It's harder to forgive ... than to hate. It's so easy to hate—and so hard to forgive.

For the Lord hears the needy and *does not despise* His who are *prisoners.*
—*Psalm 69:33*

JANUARY 15, 2024

If Ortiz's declarations prove true, his case may ascend to the Supreme Court and potentially be dismissed on a technicality, as exemplified by legal precedents such as *Minnick v. Mississippi, Edwards v. Arizona*, and the impactful ruling by D.C. Superior Court Judge Henry H. Kennedy Jr. in the *Green* case.

Justice Antonin Scalia dissented, writing that there was no justification for creating a rebuttable presumption that an accused has not waived his right to counsel after invoking that right. Chief Justice William H. Rehnquist joined in the dissent.

—*Justice Antonin Scalia*

JANUARY 19, 2024

"The president of the company responsible for recording the confession video must furnish an unaltered complete copy to ascertain whether Ortiz requested legal representation and was denied it on three occasions. Ortiz vehemently proclaims that he sought legal counsel but was refused. Where are the comprehensive videos or bodycam footage from the scene indicating that officers did not access Ortiz's locked glove compartment, remove his firearm, insert a magazine, and leave the firearm on the door panel? Will the full truth ever come to light, or will it remain concealed? Who tampered with the interrogation video, and where are the original recordings?"

JANUARY 20, 2024

As per Federico Calderon's trial testimony, Juan David Ortiz's complete deposition is archived on back-end servers. Calderon indicated that specific segments could be transferred to a CD upon request. During a Zoom status hearing on January 7, 2021, at 3:00 p.m., ADA Joaquin Rodriguez stated that a continuous interview video could not be generated due to software limitations. Ortiz recalled that during this hearing, Rodriguez referenced an email from Calderon where Chris Kubasik, CEO of L3 Technologies, conveyed that a continuous interview was unfeasible. This discrepancy prompts inquiries into the availability and completeness of the interview video. The audio quality was erratic, fluctuating in volume. L3 Technologies, formerly L-3 Communications Holdings, is overseen by Chairman and CEO Michael T. Strianese, and CEO and President Christopher E. Kubasik.

JD: During that hearing, ADA Joaquin Rodriguez read an email from Calderon—where the CEO of L3 Technologies, Chris Kubasik, informs Calderon that a continuous interview cannot be produced.

Which is it? Is the interview video complete and accessible, or is it not? Why are we not permitted to view the entire recording? What could they be concealing? This raises my curiosity about seeing the unedited video. The audio quality was abysmal, fluctuating in volume throughout.

The company in question is L3 Technologies, previously known as L-3 Communications Holdings. Michael T. Strianese serves as the Chairman and CEO, while Christopher E. Kubasik holds the positions of CEO and President.

JD: On the day that ADA Josh Davila quit ... and didn't come back from a break—or the day before, Joel Perez said super loud, "We want a mistrial." Judge Hale denied it. It had to do with Davila questioning a witness about the firearm storage. My former attorney (Joel Perez) is super smart. He is lazy, but not an idiot.

Webb County was going to let the time expire ... so I wouldn't get an appeal. Judge Hale's office said that Judge Hale believed that I didn't want to file an appeal, even though it came out on national news of me saying "yes" ... that I wanted to appeal my case. Webb County Jail put me back in a gown and didn't let me keep my Bible.

Author: I know Joel Perez tried a case—Joshua Michael Lopez was found not guilty by insanity in the 2014 killing of Elmendorf Police Chief Michael Pimentel. "He was not sane," Perez said. "Under the law, you need the act but you need the guilty mind, and not guilty by reason of insanity is, the guy didn't have a guilty mind. I have never had it happen in a capital murder, in 30 years that I have been a lawyer. So, it is a rare event." In 2015, District Attorney Nico LaHood decided not to seek the death penalty for the 28-year-old. Lopez will be sent to a state hospital to be evaluated. If the doctors do find that he is not a danger to himself or the community, then he will be a free man. It is not yet known how long he will be there. It all depends on the assessment of the mental health experts.

Author: Had you not joined the Navy and gone to war, would you still have PTSD right now?

JD: No ... I wouldn't. But I was in the Navy and Border Patrol for most of my life. That's all I know.

Author: Are you getting any sort of treatment ... like seeing a psychiatrist or taking any medication at TDCJ (Texas Department of Criminal Justice)?

JD: No ... I'm not. There are several veterans and former law enforcement like me—here where I'm at.

Author: They need to change the system, especially how we treat our veterans. You are supposed to get rehabilitation. You belong in a State Hospital ... not where you are at.

JANUARY 23, 2024

A drug rehabilitation facility, ROOTS Recovery Center, has finally opened in Laredo, offering a detox clinic intended to serve 750 individuals annually. This initiative aims to provide a much-needed refuge for those seeking recovery. Observing the impact of this facility will be crucial, given the significant demand for such services in the area.

Juan David Ortiz requested legal representation on three occasions. The anticipation for the release of the full, unedited interrogation video persists. Ortiz adamantly avows that his due process and constitutional rights have been violated. It is paramount to recognize that the Constitution of the United States, as the supreme law, safeguards fundamental rights throughout the criminal justice process. Any infringement by the government on these rights is impermissible.

FEBRUARY 19, 2024

I pledged to Ortiz that I would relay his truth, a commitment I am bound to uphold. Reflecting on the plight of war veterans with PTSD, many of whom have been prescribed Paxil by the VA, I am troubled by the government's continued allowance of Paxil despite its long-standing issues since the late 1980s. The persistence of this drug on the market, driven by profit and greed, continues to claim and devastate lives.

Every story has dual perspectives. My quest was to uncover Ortiz's truth, to decipher the enigma behind his actions. I have succeeded in this endeavor, gaining insight into Ortiz's perspective. The simplistic portrayal of Ortiz as merely a killer was insufficient for me. Future publications and media stories will emerge, but it is crucial to remember that I alone possess Ortiz's authorization to articulate his truth. Other accounts aim to sensationalize the narrative for notoriety, failing to genuinely investigate Ortiz's version of events.

I am convinced that Paxil, alcohol, and war-induced PTSD were catalysts for Ortiz's serial murders. When discussing "HIV," Ortiz exhibits significant distress. It is important to reiterate that Ortiz does not have HIV, Hepatitis C, or any sexually transmitted disease.

My personal fear of HIV, Hepatitis C, and other diseases compels me to avoid risky behavior. Should I contract such diseases, I would choose celibacy and isolation. The prevalence of HIV and Hepatitis C in Laredo, Texas, and the silent transmission of these lethal diseases, raises grave concerns.

JD: How many people did they take down?

Author: I find myself contemplating the prevalence of HIV and Hepatitis C within the population of Laredo, Texas. Specifically, I question the number of individuals living with these infections and the extent to which these diseases are being transmitted, potentially resulting in fatal outcomes. How many individuals, either knowingly or unknowingly, are contributing to the spread of these lethal diseases, effectively committing acts of murder through their transmission?

The risks associated with relationships, whether from casual encounters or infidelity within marriage, seem inescapable. The fear of contracting these diseases looms large, regardless of one's marital status. You're damned if you do (be a devoted wife) and damned if you don't (stay single).

If I had been his wife, I would have installed hidden cameras in our house to capture him in the act. Upon discovering the evidence, I would have immediately driven back from San Antonio to confront him.

Had I been Ortiz's wife, his actions would have profoundly hurt me. I would have likely pursued him with the aid of friends or a private investigator to gather evidence for a divorce. He would have faced my wrath before engaging with any sex worker. Women often possess an uncanny ability to uncover the secrets of their partners. I would have sensed his deceitful behavior and confronted him. Ortiz jested that I might have gone "Jodi Arias" on him, to which I responded, "More like Lorena Bobbitt; Jodi Arias is Burgos's girlfriend," no pun intended.

In conclusion, this narrative underscores the complex interplay of mental health, medication, and personal choices in understanding the tragic events surrounding Juan David Ortiz.

CONCLUSION

MARCH 29, 2024

Juan David Ortiz engaged in regular prayer and Bible reading, expressing a particular affinity for the Prophet Jeremiah. He fervently interceded on my behalf, supplicating for my courage in authoring this exposé, which aims to unveil the corruption perpetrated by rogue actors in his case and to articulate his personal narrative. JD demonstrates profound familiarity with biblical scripture.

THE COOKIE

Inquiries regarding JD's engagement with sex workers on San Bernardo Ave elicited contemplation from him, followed by his candid response: "I did a lot of stupid shit." The query took him by surprise, prompting an unguarded admission of past indiscretions.

Steve Harvey contends that a woman must understand how a man expresses his affection, focusing on what he terms the "three P's": "We profess, we provide and we protect" (Harvey, 2009). According to Harvey, "profess" denotes claiming the woman, followed by providing for her and safeguarding her. Harvey emphasizes the significance of sex, colloquially referred to as "the cookie," which he identifies as a crucial component in relationships: "It's critical," he insists, "It's one of the three things that a man has to have. A man has to have love, support, and the cookie. If any one of those three things is missing in the relationship, he's going to go get it somewhere else" (Harvey, 2009).

Steve Harvey differentiates between men and women regarding extramarital affairs, stating that for men, such encounters are often devoid of emotional attachment or sentimental implications: "Once we shower and wash off, we cool. Please know that about a man. If he's going to cheat, it has nothing to do with his emotional attachment to you or his feelings for you" ("Steve Harvey answers relationship questions," 2009).

JD, despite media portrayals, maintained his affection for his wife and harbored no emotional connections with any of the sex workers, as he communicated with me.

According to Steve Harvey, there exist several significant reasons why men engage in infidelity, although none of these reasons justify such behavior. The top five reasons identified include: first, the ability to engage in infidelity; second, the perception of being able to evade detection; third, a lack of personal fulfillment or uncertainty regarding ideal partnerships; fourth, dissatisfaction with the current state of affairs in the domestic sphere; and fifth, the availability of willing female counterparts ("Steve Harvey answers relationship questions," 2009).

"Once a cheater, always a cheater?" This age-old adage does not universally hold, as argued by Steve Harvey. According to Harvey (2009), "Men have the capacity for transformation. Occasionally, the forfeiture of something significant triggers a paradigm shift. ... I have evolved beyond my former self."

To All the Men and Women Out There:

If your needs are unmet in your current relationship, consider divorce and seek a new partnership that fully satisfies your emotional and physical desires, thus preventing the pursuit of satisfaction from sex workers. Ensure you are informed about the medications prescribed by your physician and any substances you consume. Promptly inform your medical practitioner if you experience feelings of suicide or homicidal tendencies.

A Message To All Women:

It is imperative that you never allow others to dictate your worth; only you possess the agency to make that determination. Your inherent value transcends external judgments. Steve Harvey states, "If you're a secretary, you're a secretary. If you're a nail tech, you're a nail tech. If you're a hooker, you're a hooker. You determine what you're worth," he says. "You should have romance with a man because of the way he treats you. You don't have romance with a man because of what he buys you" ("Steve Harvey answers relationship questions," 2009).

CORRUPTION IN THIS CASE

Ortiz's claims regarding the violation of his rights—specifically his repeated requests for legal counsel, as evidenced by the unedited confession video—and the unlawful search of his vehicle (conducted without a search warrant) compel us to dismiss his case, given that the evidence procured is tainted by the "fruit of the poisonous tree" doctrine. I hold a steadfast belief in the Constitution, which upholds the rights of Ortiz as an American citizen.

It is imperative that we acquire the unedited version of Ortiz's confession video from the president of L3 Technologies, formerly known as L-3 Communications Holdings. This acquisition is crucial for ascertaining Ortiz's narrative. Where are the national investigative journalists when we need them? Are they apprehensive about confronting Ortiz's truth and the potential revelations? The company in question is L3 Technologies, with Michael T. Strianese serving as Chairman/CEO and Christopher E. Kubasik as CEO and President.

I wish to emphasize that my commentary is not a critique of District Attorney Isidro "Chilo" Alaniz. On a personal level, I find him to be a congenial and charismatic individual. My focus here is to present Juan David Ortiz's account of the events. This account represents Ortiz's interpretation of his experience and his perceived truth. It also aligns with my own experiences and understanding of Juan David Ortiz.

There is a concerning precedent involving the Webb County Sheriff's Office, which has previously disposed of critical evidence, including videos. This raises the question: did they repeat this misconduct in Ortiz's case?

On April 25, the county settled a wrongful death lawsuit for $1.325 million in the case of Luis Alberto "Albert" Barrientos Jr., who succumbed to a treatable infection while in pre-trial detention at the jail, following a prolonged neglect of his medical needs, according to the nonprofit legal advocacy group Public Justice. The lawsuit, filed in May 2020 on behalf of Nelda Nuncio, Barrientos' mother, was a response to this egregious oversight (Rodriguez, 2023).

Barrientos had been incarcerated on June 26, 2018, on charges including aggravated assault with a deadly weapon, criminal mischief, and theft of property. "We are proud to have secured one of the largest public settlements in Webb County and to have achieved a measure of justice for the Nuncio/Barrientos family," stated Ron Rodriguez, lead counsel for the family. "We remain committed to the relentless pursuit of justice, advocating for the civil rights of the injured, and working to ensure safety within our community and nation." Nicholls added, "The court's decision correctly ruled that the jailer defendants were not entitled to qualified immunity at the motion to dismiss stage, sending a clear message to public officials that they cannot evade the civil justice system to shield themselves from wrongdoing." Regrettably, Barrientos' case is not an isolated instance (Rodriguez, 2023).

"Barrientos was not the only pre-trial detainee to perish at the jail due to the deliberate indifference of public officials. Less than 24 hours following Barrientos' death, another inmate in the same cell also succumbed to a medical condition. Additionally, Public Justice previously represented the family of Rafael Solis, who was beaten to death by jailers at Webb County Jail in 2009. None of these individuals were convicted of crimes and were incarcerated solely due to their inability to afford bail, highlighting the systemic injustices of the cash bail system and the human rights abuses that occur when jails operate with impunity" (Rodriguez, 2023).

A LITTLE PROFILING

In my interactions with Ortiz, he expressed a profound belief that he does not belong in prison. He contends that his incarceration stems from violations of his rights by corrupt law enforcement and prosecutorial misconduct driven by political motives. Ortiz maintained that he believed he was serving a greater good in Laredo. He has refrained from discussing the specifics of the murders, as he is currently appealing his conviction.

JD: I like to pull over on the side of the road and have sex. I'm spontaneous like that.

Author: Okay ...

JD: If I had seen you swimming laps in your swimsuit, I would have told you that I wanted to have sex and taken you to my house. I would want you to sit on my lap.

Author: But you are married ... Your family lived there.

Ortiz expressed a preference for spontaneity, often stopping by the roadside to engage in sexual activities. Additionally, he mentioned his inclination to invite me to his home for the same purpose, although I reminded him of his marital status. He explicitly articulated a desire for me to sit on his lap. These statements align precisely with Erika Peña's (sex worker) testimony during his trial, showcasing a consistent *modus operandi*. Ortiz continues to seek what he describes as the "girlfriend experience," emphasizing his ongoing need for affection and intimacy.

JD: One of them had her kids taken away and wouldn't even take care of her kids.

Author: Yeah ... but people aren't looking at that. It doesn't matter to the public.

JD mentioned that one of the women (victims executed) had her children removed from her care and that she did not adequately fulfill her parental responsibilities. He did not specify which woman he was referring to, but his tone suggested he was deeply affected by the subject. It seems that the concept of being a responsible parent and providing proper care for one's children is a significant trigger for him, likely stemming from his own childhood experiences.

Two distinct personas emerged in Ortiz's behavior. One is characterized by PTSD, anxiety, and panic attacks, marked by a commendable personal record and a stable, religious life, including an almost 20-year marriage (half of his life). The other persona, influenced by Paxil, engaged in seeking sex workers rather than spiritual guidance. This second persona exhibited signs of emotional blunting, and possibly mania and psychosis. Under the influence of Paxil, Ortiz's behavior drastically altered; he became a different individual, responsible for the murder of four women. He finds it deeply uncomfortable to discuss Paxil and insists that his appeal must focus on procedural errors rather than the influence of Paxil, which he asserts cannot be a basis for his appeal.

I surveyed fifteen men to ascertain whether they would permit a prostitute to enter their homes—where their spouses and children reside—to engage in heroin use followed by sexual activities. Each respondent unequivocally rejected the proposition, deeming it inherently irrational.

Juan David Ortiz knew the Bible; however, one cannot embody the principles of godliness while simultaneously engaging in adultery with prostitutes.

Ortiz was prescribed Paxil for depression, Divalproex Sodium for irritability, Trazodone for sleep disturbances, and Gabapentin for migraines. He noted that his dosages were adjusted, though he is unsure of the precise dates. Although Ortiz stated in his testimony video that he began taking these medications in mid-February 2018, he later revised this to March 2018.

To metaphorically represent the situation, consider combat PTSD and traumatic brain injury as the fuel and Paxil as the spark that ignited the conflagration—this analogy most accurately depicts the dynamics involved.

APPEAL

According to court records, the trial court properly denied the motion to suppress the statements and confessions made by Appellant and the search of his truck. His two issues on appeal are overruled. The trial court's judgment is affirmed.

JEFF ALLEY, Chief Justice

May 15, 2024

Before Alley, C.J., Palafox and Soto, JJ.

MESSAGE OF THIS BOOK

The central message of this book emphasizes that the VA must cease using combat veterans as experimental subjects for pharmaceutical companies. The mental health and medication histories of combat veterans should be thoroughly examined by defense attorneys in capital cases from the outset. Moreover, Paxil is a dangerous drug that has been linked to homicide and suicide, underscoring the need for public education about SSRIs, particularly Paxil, to prevent further harm.

The moral of this narrative is to convey a critical message: to preserve lives by avoiding Paxil medication, rather than merely to generate revenue through a captivating serial killer tale. This raises important questions: Who will be Paxil's next victim? How many lives must be sacrificed before these pills are removed from the market? Since its introduction in 1992, Paxil has been wreaking havoc—propelled by the billion-dollar interests of the top 1 percent.

IN THE MAKING

In crafting this book, I have gained considerable insights as both an author and a researcher. My approach was influenced by *Conversations with a Killer* and *Bridget Jones's Diary*, blending these styles to create a unique narrative. I adopted a method similar to Stephen King's, where chapters evolved organically during the writing process. The inclusion of legal, psychological, and related case information was crucial to substantiate my research.

I have made a conscious effort to present Juan David Ortiz as a multifaceted individual rather than a mere criminal. He is not the monstrous figure depicted by sensationalist media but a human being with a complex story. Ortiz himself contributed to the manuscript, removing inaccurate media portrayals. I aimed to infuse personality into this book to engage readers, avoiding a monotonous or impersonal tone.

Had I chosen to focus solely on the case without incorporating Ortiz's personal reflections, I could have relied on court transcripts or existing media coverage. However, I sought to explore Ortiz's own narrative, an endeavor requiring significant trust and rapport, which distinguishes this work from conventional portrayals.

Despite numerous media attempts to interview Ortiz, he declined all offers, and my efforts to reach these media personnel were unsuccessful. This rejection may stem from their resentment towards Ortiz's openness with me. Establishing this connection and presenting Ortiz's perspective involves a particular skill set, differing from the more straightforward task of critiquing him.

This book strives to be as raw and authentic as possible, incorporating my notes and Ortiz's direct statements. Engaging in a conversation-based book is inherently unpredictable; the accuracy of his words is paramount. Readers deserve an unfiltered portrayal of Ortiz and his experiences.

CRITICS

This book may not be for everyone. Some will focus solely on its perceived flaws, neglecting the significant value it offers, despite their inability to produce a comparable work themselves.

"It's easier to criticize than to create."

—*Linda Rappoport*

"It's better to create something that others criticize than to create nothing and criticize others."

—*Ricky Gervais*

"There are people out there who provide constructive criticism and I thank them. Then there are people who criticize solely because it makes *them* feel smarter. The latter group doesn't get to me because I know the effort I put into my work. The easiest job in the world is to be an arm-chair-critic. Try creating your own work. Any fool can criticize, condemn and complain and most fools do."

—*Benjamin Franklin*

JUST MERCY

After reading Bryan Stevenson's book *Just Mercy*, I find consolation in knowing that my approach to extending "mercy" aligns with that of the Equal Justice Initiative. The media's portrayal of me as an anomaly for not condemning Ortiz only reinforces my commitment to authenticity over sensationalism. The only individual I see genuinely advocating for Juan David Ortiz is Bryan Stevenson of the Equal Justice Initiative (EJI). The film *Just Mercy* chronicles Stevenson's efforts, and I was profoundly moved by his work. Meeting Bryan Stevenson—a modern-day hero—would be a tremendous honor.

As Bryan Stevenson poignantly states:

"The death penalty is not about whether people deserve to die for the crimes they commit. The real question of capital punishment in this country is, Do we deserve to kill? The true measure of our character is how we treat the poor, the disfavored, the accused, the incarcerated, and the condemned. Capital punishment means those without the capital get the punishment. Why do we want to kill all the broken people? Mercy is just when it is rooted in hopefulness and freely given. Mercy is most empowering, liberating, and transformative when it is directed at the undeserving. The people who haven't earned it, who haven't even sought it, are the most meaningful recipients of our compassion. I told them that if someone tells a lie, that person is not *just* a liar. If you take something that does not belong to you, you're not *just* a thief. Even if you kill someone, you're not *just* a killer. We need conviction in our hearts. This man taught me how to stay hopeful, because I now know that hopelessness is the enemy of justice. Each of us is more than the worst thing we've ever done." (Stevenson, 2014, p. 289).

PRESCRIPTION FOR HOMICIDE

Had Ortiz undergone a divorce, refrained from taking Paxil for his PTSD, sought a more competent psychiatrist for an appropriate medication regimen, and found a new partner who could fulfill his sexual needs—or provided him with "the cookie"—he likely would not have been on San Bernardo Avenue seeking companionship and sexual services from sex workers. Indeed, it often seems that sexual gratification—or "the cookie"—is central to these situations.

The responsibility for the tragic deaths of four women in Laredo, Texas, can be attributed to a combination of Ortiz's unresolved marital issues, his PTSD, and the administration of Paxil by the VA. Prior to this period, Ortiz maintained a clean record and displayed no such disruptive behavior. The onset of his troubling actions coincided with the introduction of Paxil into his treatment regimen, and it was also during this time that he began frequenting prostitutes. This pattern suggests a clear cause-and-effect relationship. Ortiz had an exemplary background and professional history with no prior indications of engaging with sex workers before the introduction of Paxil.

Ortiz clearly cannot tolerate SSRIs such as Paxil. The VA psychiatrist, Dr. Shankar, should be held accountable for negligence. He failed to thoroughly research Paxil and adequately evaluate Ortiz before prescribing this medication. The pharmaceutical industry, driven by profit, often exploits veterans with PTSD as experimental subjects. The continued availability of Paxil on the market is indefensible, given the associated risks.

It is my firm belief that, had Ortiz not been prescribed Paxil, he would not have committed the murders of four sex workers. Paxil, exacerbating Ortiz's pre-existing PTSD, pushed him beyond his breaking point. The combination of his unmet sexual needs, PTSD, and Paxil contributed to the devastating outcome.

I am convinced that had Juan David Ortiz not been prescribed Paxil, he would not have committed the crimes for which he is now imprisoned. Had he received appropriate therapeutic care and the correct medication, this tragedy could have been averted. Juan David, I am profoundly sorry that the system failed you. You sought help from the VA, and now find yourself in this dire predicament—a poignant testament to the failures of our institutional support systems.

I believe if Juan David Ortiz hadn't taken the Paxil ... he wouldn't have murdered anyone.

MY PET LION

One of my esteemed professors, Dr. Haruna, once remarked, "We all possess an innate animalistic instinct. However, it is the manner in which we manage this instinct that determines our ability to coexist within society and adhere to the law. Juan David Ortiz, unfortunately, was unable to exercise such control."

Juan David Ortiz was my pet lion—no pun intended. This description captures the essence of our relationship, highlighting the significant and complex role he played in my life.

AUTHOR THOUGHTS

Juan David Ortiz's actions were egregious; however, it is crucial to recognize that illegal prostitution also constitutes a criminal offense. Additionally, failing to disclose an HIV-positive status, thereby potentially transmitting the disease, is equally unlawful. Had the legal system been properly enforced, the victims would not have engaged in illegal prostitution on San Bernardo Avenue, and Ortiz might not have committed the murders.

It is my conviction that Juan David Ortiz should have been declared "Not Guilty by Reason of Temporary Insanity" and should be placed in a state hospital or mental institution. As a decorated combat veteran who served his country, Ortiz suffers from PTSD and TBI resulting from his military service. Contrary to the misconception that Ortiz would be free to roam the streets, placement in a state mental institution would ensure he receives the mental health treatment he is currently lacking. Given his service in the Iraq War, the least we can do is provide him with appropriate care in a facility that caters to his needs.

Paxil, a selective serotonin reuptake inhibitor, appears to have been a significant factor in Juan David Ortiz's commission of the murders. Given Ortiz's status as a war veteran, he should be housed in a state hospital rather than a correctional facility, particularly since the Department of Veterans Affairs had prescribed him Paxil for his PTSD. The defense counsel in Ortiz's trial was notably ineffective, failing to address the impact of Paxil on his actions. It is lamentable how our nation treats its veterans, especially those who have sacrificed so much and are subsequently failed by the system meant to protect them.

The debate surrounding Ortiz's access to mental health treatment for his PTSD and TBI should not be contentious.

Shouldn't we, as a society, advocate for the rehabilitation of veterans suffering from such conditions? Why should the prosecution, judge, or jury deny him this essential treatment?

We face a mental health crisis and a pervasive drug addiction problem. The solution for those who are mentally ill, drug-addicted, or homeless is to provide comprehensive rehabilitation to address these issues. We must either construct state hospitals and mental institutions to accommodate our most vulnerable populations or risk their presence on the streets. Addressing these problems requires more than temporary fixes; it necessitates a commitment to rehabilitation. We cannot afford to discard our combat veterans without offering them a path to recovery.

Let us not forget that the fact that an individual is struggling with addiction, homelessness, or engages in prostitution does not justify the transmission of HIV, Hepatitis C, or other communicable diseases to the public. Such actions are not only morally reprehensible but also constitute a criminal offense. In Texas, individuals diagnosed with HIV, Hepatitis C, or other communicable diseases are legally prohibited from participating in prostitution.

I am deeply disillusioned and appalled by the manner in which our government, the Department of Veterans Affairs (VA), and the legal system treat our combat veterans. We send them to war, only to abandon them upon their return, burdened with post-traumatic stress disorder (PTSD) and traumatic brain injury (TBI). Subsequently, they are relegated to the VA, where they are frequently prescribed selective serotonin reuptake inhibitors (SSRIs) such as Paxil, a drug provided by pharmaceutical companies with vested interests and government contracts. The VA's approach appears to revolve around maintaining veterans as recurring clients, ostensibly to perpetuate the cycle of medication. In the billion-dollar pharmaceutical industry, a sick patient is a profitable patient. Not all SSRIs are beneficial; some are designed to perpetuate illness rather than alleviate it.

Furthermore, the legal system fails to acknowledge PTSD as a legitimate mental illness. Lawyers often neglect to address this issue in capital cases, leading to unjust convictions and indefinite imprisonment of our combat veterans. It is imperative that we overhaul this system and enact new legislation to safeguard the rights of our veterans. PTSD must be formally recognized as a mental illness, and the legal framework should mandate that veterans facing capital charges be evaluated and, if necessary, placed in state hospitals or mental institutions.

JD: I went to the VA to get help ... and look at where I ended up—

Author: Your words keep resonating with me.

After his appeal, Juan David Ortiz grew distant. A therapist informed me that Juan David cannot engage in any healthy interaction with a woman until he receives the necessary professional assistance. "Consider the reasons for his imprisonment," the therapist advised. "Unless he opens his heart to God and demonstrates a genuine desire for transformation, he will remain incapable of forming any meaningful connections with women."

I find solace in knowing that I have not wronged him; rather, I have consistently endeavored to assist him and treat him with dignity and respect, as one would treat another human being.

As a result of my profound experience with Juan David Ortiz, I have embarked on a journey to become a therapist, with a specialized focus on veterans suffering from PTSD. The impact Juan David Ortiz has had on my life has been transformative, altering the very fabric of my existence. My interactions with him on a deeply personal level have left an indelible mark, ensuring that I will never again be the same person I was before our paths crossed.

You think you know ... but you have no idea. This is the story of Juan David Ortiz ...

I conclude with this quote: "Live by the sword, die by the sword." —*Gospel of Matthew (Matthew 26:52)*

PSALM 88 (NIV)

JD mailed me this—in his first letter to me:

1. LORD, you are the God who saves me; day and night I cry out to you.

2. May my prayer come before you; turn your ear to my cry.

3. I am overwhelmed with troubles and my life draws near to death.

4. I am counted among those who go down to the pit; I am like one without strength.

5. I am set apart with the dead, like the slain who lie in the grave, whom you remember no more, who are cut off from your care.

6. You have put me in the lowest pit, in the darkest depths.

7. Your wrath lies heavily on me; you have overwhelmed me with all your waves.

8. You have taken from me my closest friends and have made me repulsive to them. I am confined and cannot escape.

9. My eyes are dim with grief. I call to you, LORD, every day; I spread out my hands to you.

10. Do you show your wonders to the dead? Do their spirits rise up and praise you?

11. Is your love declared in the grave, your faithfulness in Destruction?

12. Are your wonders known in the place of darkness or your righteous deeds in the land of oblivion?

13. But I cry to you for help, LORD; in the morning my prayer comes before you.

14. Why, LORD, do you reject me and hide your face from me?

15. From my youth I have suffered and been close to death; I have borne your terrors and am in despair.

16. Your wrath has swept over me; your terrors have destroyed me.

17. All day long they surround me like a flood; they have completely engulfed me.

18. You have taken from me friend and neighbor— darkness is my closest friend.

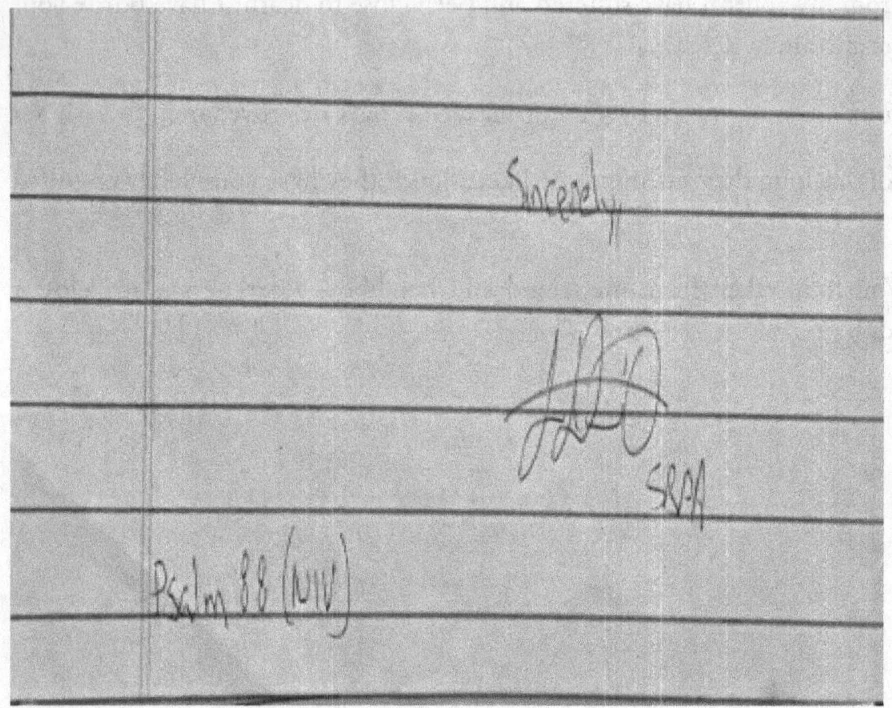

Letter from—Juan David Ortiz—his signature. *Courtesy of the author*

TWO-FACE digital oil painting art of Juan David Ortiz. *Courtesy of the author*

ACKNOWLEDGEMENTS

I would like to thank God and my family for always being there for me no matter what.

A NOTE ON SOURCES

I based—*Border Patrol Serial Killer: Conversations with Juan David Ortiz*—on exclusive interviews, conversations, messages, and letters with *Juan David Ortiz*. Furthermore, I personally attended the court hearings and trial, coupled with taking notes. For history, context, and research—I relied on other sources ...

REFERENCES

ABC News. (2001, June 6). *Jury: Paxil maker must pay $8 million.* https://abcnews.go.com/Health/story?id=117410&page=1

Allen, K. (2018, September 17). *Border patrol agent accused of killing 4 stockpiled weapons and sought 'suicide by cop': Police.* ABC News. https://abcnews.go.com/US/police-detail-texas-border-patrol-agent-allegedly-targeted/story?id=57871672

Amen, D. (n.d.). Mental Healthcare Clinic Focusing on Your Brain Health | Dr. Amen. https://www.amenclinics.com/

American Bar Association. (2016, December). *Severe mental illness and the death penalty: White paper.* Retrieved from https://www.prisonpolicy.org/scans/aba/SevereMentalIllnessandtheDeathPenalty_WhitePaper.pdf

Army reservist who killed 5 Dallas officers showed symptoms of PTSD. (2016, August 24). CBS News – Breaking news, 24/7 live streaming news & top stories. https://www.cbsnews.com/news/army-reservist-who-killed-5-dallas-officers-showed-symptoms-of-ptsd/

Associated Press. (2023, December 2). *Belief death penalty is applied unfairly shows U.S. isolation in capital punishment, report says.* NBC News. https://www.nbcnews.com/news/us-news/belief-death-penalty-applied-unfairly-shows-isolation-us-capital-punis-rcna127745

Associated Press. (2023, December 1). *Following George Floyd's murder, more believe death penalty applied unfairly.* TheGrio. https://thegrio.com/2023/12/01/following-george-floyd-murder-more-believe-death-penalty-applied-unfairly/

Barnett, N. (2020, August 27). *When transmission of HIV amounts to a crime in Texas.* Houston Criminal Defense Attorney Ned Barnett. https://www.nedbarnett.com/when-transmission-of-hiv-amounts-to-a-crime-texas/

Berghuis v. Thompkins, 560 U.S. 370 (2010). (n.d.). Justia Law.https://supreme.justia.com/cases/federal/us/560/370/

Bible gateway passage: Psalm 88 - New international version. (n.d.). Bible Gateway.https://www.biblegateway.com/passage/?search=Psalm%2088&version=NIV

Bible hub. (n.d.). Bible Hub: Search, Read, Study the Bible in Many Languages. https://biblehub.com/psalms/69-33.htm%20link.springer.com/article/10.1007/s11682-015-9385-5#citeas

Bonn, S. (2018, September 17). *Understanding pragmatic mission killers.* Psychology Today. https://www.psychologytoday.com/us/blog/wicked-deeds/201809/understanding-pragmatic-mission-killers

Border patrol agent jailed on $2.5M bond in killings of 4 women in Texas. (2018, September 16). CBS News - Breaking news, 24/7 live streaming news & top stories. https://www.cbsnews.com/news/juan-david-ortiz-border-patrol-agent-jailed-serial-killer-texas-arrested-bond-today-2018-09-16/

Boseley, S. (2001, June 11). *Murder, suicide. A bitter aftertaste for the 'wonder' depression drug.* The Guardian. https://www.theguardian.com/uk/2001/jun/11/highereducation.medicalscience

Carroll, S. (2007, April 15). *Drug cartel hires Texas teens as border hitmen.* https://www.chron.com/news/houston-texas/article/Drug-cartel-hires-Texas-teens-as-border-hitmen-1825635.php

Chandler, K. (2023, November 8). *Alabama sets January execution date using nitrogen gas.* AP News. https://apnews.com/article/death-penalty-nitrogen-hypoxia-gas-execution-efafd08559c1bf876e2f7903305ca13c

Cooke, R. (2019, May 9). *A serial killer at the border – and the women who stood up to him.* The Guardian. https://www.theguardian.com/us-news/2019/may/09/juan-david-ortiz-laredo-serial-killer-border-patrol-agent-women-stood-up-deaths

Crabtree, S. (2022, May 11). *Jury verdict: 'competent' for EC killer trial appeal.* Leader News. https://www.leader-news.com/news/article_3ec5c6b6-d0b0-11ec-a634-0b0f73e1c5cb.html

Dancyger, L. (2018, December 6). *Texas seeking death penalty for alleged border-patrol serial killer.* Rolling Stone. https://www.rollingstone.com/culture/culture-news/serial-killer-border-patrol-death-penalty-763950/

Davis, Z. (2022, October 2). *Records show findings in alleged serial killer trial after motion to suppress denied.* Laredo Morning Times. https://www.lmtonline.com/local/article/Records-show-findings-conclusions-in-alleged-17480318.php

Death Penalty Information Center. (1995, February 1). *On the Front Line: Law Enforcement Views on the Death Penalty.* https://deathpenaltyinfo.org/facts-and-research/dpic-reports/in-depth/on-the-front-line-law-enforcement-views-on-the-death-penalty

Death Penalty Information Center. (n.d.). *Arguments for and Against the Death Penalty.* https://deathpenaltyinfo.org/curriculum/high-school/about-the-death-penalty/arguments-for-and-against-the-death-penalty

Death Penalty Information Center. (n.d.). *Prosecutorial Accountability.* https://deathpenaltyinfo.org/policy-issues/prosecutorial-accountability

Death Penalty Information Center. (n.d.). *Victims' Families.* https://deathpenaltyinfo.org/policy-issues/victims-families

Deprivation of rights under color of law. (2021, May 31). Department of Justice | United States Department of Justice. https://www.justice.gov/crt/deprivation-rights-under-color-law

Dissociative identity disorder: What is it, symptoms & treatment. (n.d.). Cleveland Clinic. https://my.clevelandclinic.org/health/diseases/9792-dissociative-identity-disorder-multiple-personality-disorder

Edelman, S. (2004, September 19). *How Paxil killed our son.* New York Post. https://nypost.com/2004/09/19/how-paxil-killed-our-son/

Edwards v. Arizona. (2023, September 13). Wikipedia, the free encyclopedia. Retrieved January 15, 2024, from https://en.wikipedia.org/wiki/Edwards_v._Arizona

Emmons, D. (2023, January 25). *From persecutor to Christian: The conversion of St. Paul.* Simply Catholic. https://www.simplycatholic.com/from-persecutor-to-christian-the-conversion-of-st-paul/

Facts about the death penalty. (2018, February 8). Texas Catholic Conference. https://txcatholic.org/facts-death-penalty/

Flores, A., & Wyler, G. (2018, September 15). *A border patrol agent has been arrested for killing four women.* BuzzFeed News. https://www.buzzfeednews.com/article/adolfoflores/a-border-patrol-agent-has-been-arrested-for-killing-four

Furlong, A., & Geffen, N. (2016, December 13). *Should you be prosecuted for exposing someone to HIV?* GroundUp News. https://groundup.org.za/article/should-people-who-transmit-hiv-be-prosecuted/

Hart, B. (2018, September 16). *Border patrol officer suspected of killing four women in Texas.* Intelligencer. https://nymag.com/intelligencer/2018/09/juan-david-ortiz-border-patrol-killer.html

Harvey, S., & Millner, D. (2009). *Act like a lady, think like a man: what men really think about love, relationships, intimacy, and commitment.* New York, Amistad.

Hernandez, S. (2013, December 1). *Sex, lies and HIV: When what you don't tell your partner is a crime.* ProPublica. https://www.propublica.org/article/hiv-criminal-transmission

HIV-positive Texas man gets 15 years in prison for infecting woman. (2013, January 2). CBS News - Breaking news, 24/7 live streaming news & top stories. https://www.cbsnews.com/news/hiv-positive-texas-man-gets-15-years-in-prison-for-infecting-woman/

Hollandsworth, S. (2022, December 9). *What drove Juan David Ortiz, a respected border patrol agent, to become a serial killer?* Texas Monthly. https://www.texasmonthly.com/true-crime/what-drove-juan-david-ortiz-border-patrol-serial-murder-laredo/

Holmes, R. (1985, September). *Profiles in terror - The serial murderer*. Office of Justice Programs. https://www.ojp.gov/ncjrs/virtual-library/abstracts/profiles-terror-serial-murderer

Izaguirre, A. (2023, May 1). *DeSantis signs death penalty, crime bills as 2024 run looms.* AP News. https://apnews.com/article/death-penalty-child-rape-desantis-florida-9b03e9cd5a96f68967c3e06a299ff2a7

Jeff. (2020, February 4). *Martin Luther King, Jr.* Center on Conscience & War. https://centeronconscience.org/martin-luther-king-jr/

Johnson Law Group. (n.d.). *Is Paxil an antidepressant that kills?* SG & Singapore Map! Powered by Streetdirectory.com. https://www.streetdirectory.com/travel_guide/25478/alternative_medicine/is_paxil_an_antidepressant_that_kills.html

Josefson, D. (2001, June 16). *Jury finds drug 80% responsible for killings.* PubMed Central (PMC). https://www.ncbi.nlm.nih.gov/pmc/articles/PMC1173337/

Kalmbacher, C. (2018, September 15). *Border agent Juan David Ortiz targeted sex workers.* Law & Crime. https://lawandcrime.com/crime/border-agent-confesses-to-being-serial-killer-who-targeted-sex-workers/

LibGuides: Ethical topics: Capital punishment. (2023, May 11). https://materchristi.libguides.com/Ethical_Topics/capital_punishment

Lozano, J. (2023, December 2). *Belief death penalty is applied unfairly shows U.S. isolation in capital punishment, report says.* NBC News. https://www.nbcnews.com/news/us-news/belief-death-penalty-applied-unfairly-shows-isolation-us-capital-punis-rcna127745

Lozano, J. (2023, December 1). *For the first time, more Americans believe death penalty is applied unfairly, report finds.* PBS NewsHour. https://www.pbs.org/newshour/nation/for-the-first-time-more-americans-believe-death-penalty-is-applied-unfairly-report-finds

Madani, D., Blankstein, A., Leonard, E., & Romero, D. (2019, March 12). *California Gov. Gavin Newsom plans to halt the death penalty.* NBC News. https://www.nbcnews.com/news/us-news/gov-gavin-newsom-expected-try-end-death-penalty-california-through-n982556

Mass murder and psychiatric drugs. (n.d.). Medical Whistleblower. https://medicalwhistleblower.org/mass-murder-and-psychiatric-drugs

Miller, J. (2022, November 29). *Trial underway for Texas border patrol agent accused of murdering four sex workers.* Oxygen Official Site. https://www.oxygen.com/crime-news/border-patrol-agent-juan-david-ortiz-on-trial-for-4-murders

Minnick v. Mississippi, 498 U.S. 146 (1990). (n.d.). Justia Law. https://supreme.justia.com/cases/federal/us/498/146/

Montoya Bryan, S. (2018, September 20). *Agent accused in serial killings lived quiet suburban life.* AP News. https://apnews.com/article/0d20a9865c7140f6876168e40a6289e8

MYSA. (2011, April 10). *San Antonian still on death row after 31 years.* mysanantonio.com. https://www.mysanantonio.com/news/local/article/San-Antonian-still-on-death-row-after-31-years-1330317.php

National Academics. (2012, April 18). https://www.nationalacademies.org/news/2012/04/current-research-not-sufficient-to-assess-deterrent-effect-of-the-death-penalty

No Man of God. (2021, August 27). IMDb. https://www.imdb.com/title/tt13507778/

NotiGape. (2018, September 19). *Posible VIH pudo detonar crímenes.* NotiGAPE. https://www.notigape.com/posible-vih-pudo-detonar-crimenes/174904

Paroxetine treatment of problematic pornography use: A case series. (2016, September 1). AKJournals. https://akjournals.com/view/journals/2006/5/3/article-p529.xml

Paul, an imperfect man, used by god. (n.d.). Al Brown's. https://www.w1vtp.com/paul-used-by-God.htm

Paxil suicide lawsuits. (n.d.). Wisner Baum. https://www.wisnerbaum.com/prescription-drugs/paxil-suicide-lawsuit/

Penal code Chapter 22. Assaultive offenses. (n.d.). Texas Constitution and Statutes. https://statutes.capitol.texas.gov/Docs/PE/htm/PE.22.htm

Pirius, R. (2023, March 2). *Transmitting an STD in Texas.* www.criminaldefenselawyer.com. https://www.criminaldefenselawyer.com/resources/transmitting-std-texas.htm

Prescription drug side-effects: How they're vastly under-reported and one man's tragic, cautionary tale. (2021, October 9). CTVNews. https://www.ctvnews.ca/w5/prescription-drug-side-effects-how-they-re-vastly-under-reported-and-one-man-s-tragic-cautionary-tale-1.5616839

Prostitution charges in Texas. (2013, November 16). Varghese Summersett PLLC. https://versustexas.com/fort-worth-prostitution-lawyer/

Qualified immunity. (2024, February 5). Wikipedia, the free encyclopedia. Retrieved February 12, 2024, from

Raji, C. (2015, April 23). *Functional neuroimaging with default mode network regions distinguishes PTSD from TBI in a military veteran population.* SpringerLink. https://link.springer.com/article/10.1007/s11682-015-9385-5#citeas

Ramos, H. (2018, July 2). *Suspect found not guilty by reason of insanity in killing of Elmendorf police chief.* kens5.com. https://www.kens5.com/article/news/local/suspect-not-guilty-by-insanity-in-killing-of-elmendorf-police-chief/273-570008798

Rodriguez, C. (2019, May 7). *Star witness in serial killer case arrested on three charges.* Laredo Morning Times. https://www.lmtonline.com/local/crime/article/Star-witness-in-serial-killer-case-arrested-on-13825473.php

Rodriguez, C. (2023, May 14). *$1.3 settlement reached in wrongful death of Webb County Jail inmate.* Laredo Morning Times: Laredo TX News, Sports and Border News. https://www.lmtonline.com/local/article/wrongful-death-webb-county-jail-inmate-settled-18097693.php

Rodriguez, C. (2023, December 2). *DA Alaniz to talk challenges in serial killer case at conference.* Laredo Morning Times. https://www.lmtonline.com/local/article/da-prepares-conference-talks-challenges-serial-18528990.php

Rodriguez, C. (2023, December 11). *Star witness in USBP serial killer case arrested again.* Laredo Morning Times. https://www.lmtonline.com/local/article/star-witness-border-patrol-serial-killer-case-18547396.php

Rodriguez, C. (2023, November 22). *Star witness in USBP serial killer case arrested for assaulting LPD cop.* Laredo Morning Times. https://www.lmtonline.com/local/article/witness-usbp-serial-killer-case-charged-18509344.php

Rodriguez, C. (2024, February 8). *Former Webb County jailer faces federal charges for raping 2 inmates.* Laredo Morning Times. https://www.lmtonline.com/local/article/former-jailer-faces-federal-charges-raping-2-18656420.php

Romero, D. (2018, September 15). *Border patrol agent suspected in string of sex worker deaths in Texas.* NBC News. https://www.nbcnews.com/news/crime-courts/border-patrol-agent-suspected-texas-serial-murder-case-n909926

Salas, M. (2020, July 14). *Laredo judge denies motion to suppress confession of alleged BP serial killer.* Laredo Morning Times. https://www.lmtonline.com/local/crime/article/Judge-denies-motion-to-suppress-confession-of-15406771.php

Salas, M. (2022, October 5). *DA not seeking death penalty against alleged serial killer.* Laredo Morning Times. https://www.lmtonline.com/local/article/DA-seeking-life-without-parole-against-USBP-agent-17489632.php

Salas, M. (2022, December 2). *DA reflects on four-year journey.* Laredo Morning Times. https://www.lmtonline.com/local/article/DA-reflects-on-four-year-journey-after-Ortiz-trial-17644608.php

Salas, M. (2022, November 28). *Trial begins for alleged Laredo serial killer, ex-USBP agent.* Laredo Morning Times. https://www.lmtonline.com/local/article/Trial-begins-for-alleged-Laredo-serial-killer-17616432.php

Sengupta, S. (2023, November 28). *Erika Pena: Where is the survivor now?* The Cinemaholic. https://thecinemaholic.com/erika-pena-where-is-the-survivor-now/

Sengupta, S. (2023, September 15). *Juan David Ortiz: Where is the serial killer ex-cop now?* The Cinemaholic. https://thecinemaholic.com/juan-david-ortiz-where-is-the-serial-killer-ex-cop-now/

Silva, D. (2018, September 17). *Border patrol agent accused of serial killings wanted to 'commit suicide by cop,' officials say.* NBC News. https://www.nbcnews.com/news/us-news/border-patrol-agent-accused-serial-killings-wanted-commit-suicide-cop-n910456

Steve Harvey answers relationship questions. (2009, March 23). Oprah.com. https://www.oprah.com/relationships/steve-harvey-answers-your-relationship-questions/all

Stevenson, B. (2015). *Just mercy: a story of justice and redemption.* Spiegel & Grau trade paperback edition. New York, Spiegel & Grau.

Texas Coalition to Abolish the Death Penalty. (n.d.). *How to Address the Tough Points*. TCADP. https://tcadp.org/wp-content/uploads/2010/06/How-to-Address-the-Tough-Points.pdf

Texas Coalition to Abolish the Death Penalty. (n.d.). *Mental Illness and the Death Penalty in Texas: Know the Facts*. TCADP. https://tcadp.org/wp-content/uploads/2010/06/MIDP-Fact-Sheet-03-08.pdf

Texas Jury Sentences ex-USBP Agent Who Committed Two Murders to Life Without Parole Instead of Death. (2023, July 21). https://deathpenaltyinfo.org/news/texas-jury-sentences-ex-usbp-agent-who-committed-two-murders-to-life-without-parole-instead-of-death

Tolan, C. (2019, March 15). *Democrats in presidential race applaud California's death penalty moratorium*. The Mercury News. https://www.mercurynews.com/2019/03/14/kamala-harris-death-penalty-capital-punishment-california-2020-presidential-race/

Torry, S. (1990, December 5). *HIGH COURT RULING HITS HOME QUICKLY*. The Washington Post. https://www.washingtonpost.com/archive/local/1990/12/05/high-court-ruling-hits-home-quickly/b9f8b27c-a388-481e-9a73-b1de8c97a297/

United States v. Brignoni-Ponce. (2023, December 29). Wikipedia, the free encyclopedia. Retrieved January 19, 2024, from https://en.wikipedia.org/wiki/United_States_v._Brignoni-Ponce

United States v. Dominguez. (2015, October 21). Casetext - CoCounsel. https://casetext.com/case/united-states-v-dominguez-88

United States v. Martinez-Fuerte. (2023, September 13). Wikipedia, the free encyclopedia. Retrieved January 19, 2024, from https://en.wikipedia.org/wiki/United_States_v._Martinez-Fuerte#History

Wasteful & inefficient. (2019, December 9). Equal Justice USA. https://ejusa.org/resource/wasteful-inefficient/

Wooldridge, A. (2023, January 10). *Paxil and alcohol: Side effects & risks.* K Health. https://khealth.com/learn/medication/paxil-and-alcohol/

Young, S. (2012, November 10). *Imprisoned over HIV: One man's story.* CNN. https://www.cnn.com/2012/08/02/health/criminalizing-hiv/index.html

ABOUT THE AUTHOR

Dr. Lyzza Janette, born and raised in Laredo, Texas, currently resides in the same city. She earned her Doctor of Business Administration with a concentration in Advanced Accounting from Northcentral University (National University). Additionally, she holds a Master's Degree in Public Administration and a Bachelor's Degree in Political Science with a minor in Communications from Texas A&M International University. Dr. Janette is an alumna of the National Society of Leadership and Success and the National Scholars Honor Society and was featured on the Dean's List. She pursued studies at the esteemed Lee Strasberg Theatre and Film Institute in West Hollywood, California. Dr. Janette made an appearance on the Steve Harvey Show episode "Is It A Deal Breaker?" She possesses an ENFJ personality type and is a Taurus.

Dr. Lyzza Janette is the author of the following published scholarly source and books:

1. *The Role of Management Accounting in Hospital Management Support* (Doctoral Dissertation on ProQuest)

2. *God Saved Me From Death Row: Miguel Angel Martinez* (2nd Version)

3. *lyzza janette's diary*

4. *Butterfly*

5. *Frankie the Pug*

6. *GOD SAVED ME FROM DEATH ROW*

7. *Getting Up Even Stronger*

8. *The Girl Inside the Woman Inside Me*

Contact the author at: authorlyzzajanette@gmail.com

Dr. Lyzza Janette. *Courtesy of the author*

9 798333 023 9856